The Cambridge Introduction to
Virginia Woolf

For students of modern literature, the works of Virginia Woolf are essential reading. In her novels, short stories, essays, polemical pamphlets and in her private letters she explored, questioned and refashioned everything about modern life: cinema, sexuality, shopping, education, feminism, politics and war. Her elegant and startlingly original sentences became a model of modernist prose. This is a clear and informative introduction to Woolf's life, works, and cultural and critical contexts, explaining the importance of the Bloomsbury group in the development of her work. It covers the major works in detail, including *To the Lighthouse, Mrs Dalloway, The Waves* and the key short stories. As well as providing students with the essential information needed to study Woolf, Jane Goldman suggests further reading to allow students to find their way through the most important critical works. All students of Woolf will find this a useful and illuminating overview of the field.

JANE GOLDMAN is Senior Lecturer in English and American Literature at the University of Dundee.

Cambridge Introductions to Literature

This series is designed to introduce students to key topics and authors. Accessible and lively, these introductions will also appeal to readers who want to broaden their understanding of the books and authors they enjoy.

- Ideal for students, teachers, and lecturers
- Concise, yet packed with essential information
- Key suggestions for further reading

Titles in this series:

The Cambridge Introduction to
Virginia Woolf

JANE GOLDMAN

CAMBRIDGE
UNIVERSITY PRESS

CAMBRIDGE UNIVERSITY PRESS
Cambridge, New York, Melbourne, Madrid, Cape Town, Singapore, São Paulo

CAMBRIDGE UNIVERSITY PRESS
The Edinburgh Building, Cambridge CB2 2RU, UK

Published in the United States of America by Cambridge University Press, New York

www.cambridge.org
Information on this title: www.cambridge.org/9780521547567

First published 2006

Printed in the United Kingdom at the University Press, Cambridge

A Catalogue record for this publication is available from the British Library

ISBN-13 978-0-521-83883-2 hardback
ISBN-10 0-521-83883-5 hardback
ISBN-13 978-0-521-54756-7 paperback
ISBN-10 0-521-54756-3 paperback

Contents

Preface

Reading Virginia Woolf will change your life, may even save it. If you want to make sense of modern life, the works of Virginia Woolf remain essential reading. More than fifty years since her death, accounts of her life still set the pace for modern modes of living. Plunge (and this *Introduction* is intended to help you take the plunge) into Woolf's works – at *any* point – whether in her novels, her short stories, her essays, her polemical pamphlets, or her published letters, diaries, memoirs and journals – and you will be transported by her elegant, startling, buoyant sentences to a world where everything in modern life (cinema, sexuality, shopping, education, feminism, politics, war and so on) is explored and questioned and refashioned. 'My brain', she confides in one diary entry, 'is ferociously active' (*D3* 132); and Woolf's writing is infused with her formidably productive mental energy, with her appetite for modern life, modern people and modern art. Woolf's writing both records and shapes modern experience, modern consciousness; but it also opens up to scrutiny the process of writing itself, a process she herself frequently records, and also finds exhilarating.

She famously depicts fictional writing, in *A Room of One's Own* (1929), as 'a spider's web, attached ever so lightly perhaps, but still attached to life at all four corners'. Fictional works may, Woolf claims, 'seem to hang there complete by themselves. But when the web is pulled askew, hooked up at the edge, torn in the middle, one remembers that these webs are not spun in mid-air by incorporeal creatures, but are the work of suffering human beings, and are attached to grossly material things, like health and money and the houses we live in' (*AROO* 62–3). This *Introduction* will guide you through Woolf's writing, but also delineate for you the life of the person who produced it (her critical and cultural afterlife, too): you will be introduced, then, to both spider and web. As an appetiser to both, let us sample Woolf's fascinating account of her writing process at the heart of her writing life.

In the spring of 1927, the 35-year-old Woolf takes stock, in one brief diary entry, of her achievements to date – she has by now published five novels, including *Mrs Dalloway* (1925) and *To the Lighthouse* (1927) – as she contemplates beginning her sixth novel, *Orlando* (1928), and even enjoys glimpses of her seventh, *The Waves* (1931); at the same time, she is also knuckling down to writing the most enduringly modern, feminist manifesto, *A Room of One's Own*. Considering the shape of the work that is to become *Orlando*, she envisages that 'Everything is to be tumbled in pall mall [*sic*]. It is to be written as I write letters at the top of my speed . . . No attempt is to be made to realise the character. Sapphism is to be suggested. Satire is to be the main note – satire & wildness' (*D3* 131). But this novel is also to 'satirise' her own, previous writing:

> For the truth is I feel the need of an escapade after these serious poetic experimental books . . . I want to kick up my heels & be off. I want to embody all those innumerable little ideas & tiny stories which flash into my mind at all seasons. I think this will be great fun to write; & it will rest my head before starting the very serious, mystical poetical work which I want to come next.   (*D3* 131)

This premonition of the novel that becomes *The Waves* sets her thinking about her writing agenda for the coming months, and her own creative processes:

> Meanwhile . . . I have to write my book on fiction [*A Room of One's Own*] & that wont be done till January, I suppose. I might dash off a page or two now & then by way of experiment. And it is possible that the idea will evaporate. Anyhow this records the odd hurried unexpected way in which these things suddenly create themselves – one thing on top of another in about an hour. So I made up Jacob's Room looking at the fire at Hogarth House; so I made up The Lighthouse one afternoon in the square here.   (*D3* 131–2)

However quickly her works are conceived and 'made up', as she records here, Woolf's final published works we know to have been rigorously drafted and redrafted. Every word in every sentence on every page has been subjected to her scrutiny. Her pride in such perfectionism is evident in another diary entry: 'Dear me, how lovely some parts of The Lighthouse are! Soft & pliable, & I think deep, & never a word wrong for a page at a time' (*D3* 132). The following *Introduction* to Woolf aims to show you the main features of her web, but also to illuminate some of its finely wrought detail, too – the crucial engineering of her sentences, the devastating precision of her words. It will also consider how both spider and web have in turn been woven into decades of literary criticism and theory, and academic and popular accounts of modern culture. In short, *The Cambridge Introduction to Virginia Woolf* offers a unique combination of clear and informative entrées to the life, works, and cultural and critical contexts. As well as providing you with the essential basic facts in all these realms, it will give you the opportunity to make informed decisions about further reading in Woolf and Woolf studies. This *Introduction* owes its existence and is also dedicated to the international community of Woolf scholars, which is now so large, and its works so numerous, that it has not been possible to cite in these pages every name or contribution of significance. I would also like to thank the many students and colleagues with whom, over many happy years, I have studied Virginia Woolf's writings – at the Universities of Dundee, Glasgow and Edinburgh, and at the Scottish Universities' International Summer School.

'We are the words; we are the music;
we are the thing itself'   (*MOB* 72)

Abbreviations

Quotations will be cited in parentheses in the text by page number, or by volume and page number. Any inconsistencies and idiosyncrasies of spelling, syntax and punctuation are Woolf's own.

AROO	*A Room of One's Own* (London: Hogarth, 1929)
BA	*Between the Acts* (London: Hogarth, 1941)
CE	*Collected Essays*, 4 vols., ed. Leonard Woolf (London: Chatto & Windus, 1967)
CH	Robin Majumdar and Allen McLaurin (eds.), *Virginia Woolf: The Critical Heritage* (London: Routledge & Kegan Paul, 1975)
CSF	*The Complete Shorter Fiction of Virginia Woolf*, ed. Susan Dick, 2nd edn (London: Hogarth, 1989)
D1–5	*The Diary of Virginia Woolf (1915–1941)*, 5 vols., ed. Anne Olivier Bell and Andrew McNeillie (London: Hogarth, 1977–84)
E1–4	*The Essays of Virginia Woolf*, vols. 1–4 (of 6), ed. Andrew McNeillie (London: Hogarth, 1986–94)
F	*Flush: A Biography* (London: Hogarth, 1933)
JR	*Jacob's Room* (London: Hogarth, 1922)
L1–6	*The Letters of Virginia Woolf (1888–1941)*, 6 vols., ed. Nigel Nicolson and Joanne Trautman (London: Hogarth, 1975–80)
LAW	Margaret Llewellyn-Davies (ed.), *Life As We Have Known It by Co-Operative Working Women* (London: Hogarth, 1931)
LS	*The London Scene* (London: Snowbooks, 2004)
LWL	Leonard Woolf, *The Letters of Leonard Woolf*, ed. Frederick Spotts (London: Weidenfeld & Nicolson, 1989)
M	*The Moment and Other Essays* (London: Hogarth, 1947)
MD	*Mrs Dalloway* (London: Hogarth, 1925)
MOB	*Moments of Being*, ed. Jeanne Schulkind, 2nd edn (London: Hogarth, 1985)
ND	*Night and Day* (London: Duckworth, 1919)
O	*Orlando: A Biography* (London: Hogarth, 1928)

TG	*Three Guineas* (London: Hogarth, 1938)
TL	*To the Lighthouse* (London: Hogarth, 1927)
TLH	*To the Lighthouse: The Original Holograph Draft*, ed. Susan Dick (Toronto and London: University of Toronto Press, 1983)
VBL	Vanessa Bell, *The Selected Letters of Vanessa Bell*, ed. Regina Marler (London: Bloomsbury, 1993)
VO	*The Voyage Out* (London: Duckworth, 1915)
VWB1–2	Quentin Bell, *Virginia Woolf: A Biography*, 2 vols. (London: Hogarth, 1972)
VWIL	Julia Briggs, *Virginia Woolf: An Inner Life* (London: Penguin, 2005)
VWL	Hermione Lee, *Virginia Woolf* (London: Chatto & Windus, 1996)
W	*The Waves* (London: Hogarth, 1931)
WD	*A Writer's Diary*, ed. Leonard Woolf (London: Hogarth, 1953)
Y	*The Years* (London: Hogarth, 1937)

Life

It is quite a responsibility to relate even the bare facts of Virginia Woolf's life, given the sometimes explosively diverging accounts of it in circulation. There are numerous published biographies of Woolf, as well as various collective Bloomsbury ones, a number of which will be briefly considered in Chapter Two. And sketches and snippets concerning Woolf's life crop up in all sorts of places, from Hollywood films to fashion magazine spreads. Leaving aside for the moment such fleeting, and often wholly misleading, cultural appropriations of Woolf's life and persona, each serious biography presents Woolf in a different light, and some offer quite differing views of everything from her writing habits to her relationships, her sexuality, her illness and her suicide. The daughter of the literary biographer Leslie Stephen, and close friend of the innovative biographer of the Victorians, Lytton Strachey, Woolf herself put forward, in 'The New Biography' (1927) (reviewing work by another biographer acquaintance, Harold Nicolson), her own memorable theory of biography, encapsulated in her phrase 'granite and rainbow'. 'Truth' she envisions 'as something of granite-like solidity', and 'personality as something of rainbow-like intangibility', and 'the aim of biography', she proposes, 'is to weld these two into one seamless whole' (*E4* 473). The following short biographical account of Woolf will attempt to keep to the basic granite-like facts that Woolf novices need to know, while also occasionally attending in brief to the more elusive, but equally relevant, matter of rainbow-like personality.

Woolf did not publish – or indeed, write – a formal autobiography, but she did write, for her own circle of Bloomsbury intimates, a number of brief memoirs, reminiscences and autobiographical sketches, most of which have been published posthumously. Her letters, diaries and journals have also been published (in twelve volumes in all), and constitute a rich body of autobiographical writing. Although the diaries and letters are often plundered (as they will be below), for 'the insights they afford into Woolf's writing, or . . . into Woolf herself', or, indeed, into the many notable contemporaries she knew, corresponded with and encountered, they are works also to be 'read in their own right'.[1] In her most sustained document of reminiscence, 'A Sketch of the Past', written between the summer of 1939 and the winter of 1940, Woolf considers 'the memoir writer's difficulties', concluding that 'one of the reasons why . . . so many are failures' is that they 'leave out the person to whom things happened'. Memoir writers often describe what happened, she observes, 'but they do not say what the person was like to whom it happened' (*MOB* 73). For this reason she begins her own memoir without factual preamble, but with two of her earliest 'colour-and-sound memories' of childhood. The first is the sight of the pattern of 'purple and red and blue' flowers on her mother's black dress as she sat on her knee while they travelled 'either in a train or in an omnibus'. The second, 'most important', and – for her – foundational, memory is of hearing from her bed 'waves breaking . . . over the beach' at St Ives, and hearing at the same time her window blind 'draw its little acorn across the floor as the wind blew the blind out'. She remembers this experience of 'the waves and the acorn on the blind' producing 'the purest ecstasy I can conceive', and she is fond of describing it to herself, she confesses, as 'the feeling . . . of lying in a grape and seeing through a film of semi-transparent yellow' (*MOB* 73–4).

This surreal, yet tender, self-portrait of the writer as a young sensate grape seed is a brilliant introduction because it encourages us momentarily to clear our mind of whatever knowledge or preconceptions about Woolf we may bring to our reading of her life and her works. It encourages us to identify with the primary sensations of rhythmic sound and colour of early infancy, and to compare our own such personal, and distinct, 'colour-and-sound memories' with hers. A dialogue has begun between Woolf's writing and her reader. 'If life has a base that it stands upon,' Woolf writes, 'if it is a bowl that one fills and fills and fills – then my bowl without a doubt stands upon this memory' (*MOB* 73). On what memory does your bowl stand? 'A Sketch of the Past' connects such memories to the material facts of Woolf's life, too. She questions how these subjective moments themselves stand on the supposedly more tangible fabric of historical, political, social and familial experience. Woolf acknowledges the granite-like facts that she 'was born into a large connection, born . . . of well-to-do parents, born into a very communicative, literate, letter writing, visiting, articulate, late nineteenth century world'; but she does not know, she says, 'how much of this, or what part of this, made me feel what I felt in the nursery at St Ives. I do not know how far I differ from other people' (*MOB* 73). Woolf urges us to consider what experiences are formative for the individual, and for the writer; and what experiences may be common to us all.

Towards the close of her memoir, she records glimpses of darker historical events unfolding as she writes and reflects on her primal childhood moments: 'Yesterday (18 August 1940) five German raiders passed so close over Monks House that they brushed the tree at the gate. But being alive today, and having a waste hour on my hands – for I am writing fiction; and cannot write after twelve – I will go on with this loose story' (*MOB* 137). Woolf wrote her final novel, *Between the Acts* (1941), and her final memoir, then, under a sky darkened by warfare; and under such a sky her writing constitutes, for her then and us now, a life-affirming act. Whatever other events and facts you discover about Woolf's life, whatever your response to her work, her first vital memories become a powerful touchstone. Whatever opinion you come to form of her life or of her writing, bear in mind that she remembers what it was like to sit on her mother's knee and see the colours of her dress, what it was like to lie in bed and hear waves and a window blind moving, the blissful feeling of lying at the centre of a luminous yellow grape. She knows what it is to remember and record such moments during the darkest of times. Her genius lies in seeing that this is the most important kind of communication to make.

1882–1909

Virginia Woolf was born Adeline Virginia Stephen on 25 January 1882, at 22 Hyde Park Gate, in Kensington, London. She was indeed 'born into a large connection'. Her father was the distinguished Victorian author, critic and Alpinist, Sir Leslie Stephen (1832–1904), editor of the *Cornhill Magazine* (1871–82), of the *Dictionary of National Biography* (1882–90) and of the *Alpine Journal* (1868–72), who counted Thomas Hardy, Henry James and George Meredith among his friends. Leslie Stephen came from a long line of Puritan philanthropists, known as the Clapham Sect. His father, and Woolf's grandfather, was Sir James Stephen (1789–1859), Regius Professor of Modern History at Cambridge University and noted Counsel to the Colonial Office and Board of Trade, who framed the bill to abolish slavery in 1833. Leslie Stephen was educated at Eton and Trinity Hall, Cambridge, where he became a deacon in 1855 and then parson (in the Church of England) in 1859. By 1862 he had lost his religious faith and so resigned his post as a tutor at

Trinity Hall; he left Cambridge in 1864. He made a formative journey to America in 1863 and witnessed at first hand the turmoil of the Civil War. He was on the side of the Unionists and greatly admired Lincoln. He married Minnie, the daughter of William Makepeace Thackeray, in 1867, and their daughter Laura was born in 1870. Minnie died in 1875. Three years after her death, Stephen married Woolf's mother.

Her mother was Julia Prinsep Stephen (1846–95), who was born Julia Prinsep Jackson, in India, the daughter of John and Maria Jackson. Her maternal grandmother, and Woolf's great-grandmother and namesake, was Adeline (1793–1845), daughter of Antoine Chevalier de L'Etang and Thérèse Blin Grincourt, who married James Pattle (1775–1845) of the Bengal Civil Service; this marriage was one of Woolf's 'favourite pieces of family history' (*VWL* 88). Julia Jackson, who returned with her mother to England in 1848, became a renowned beauty, admired and painted by Edward Burne-Jones and G. F. Watts in her youth, and photographed by her esteemed maternal aunt Julia Margaret Cameron (1815–97). The artists William Holman-Hunt and Thomas Woolner were among her disappointed suitors when she married, in 1867, Herbert Duckworth (1833–70) with whom she had three children, George (1868–1934), Stella (1869–97) and Gerald (1870–1937). She was widowed after three years shortly before the birth of her third child. Leslie Stephen was forty-six when he married Julia Duckworth in 1878. She was thirty-two. He had been a widower for three years, she a widow for eight. Leslie brought one child, Julia three, to their marriage. Virginia was the third of four children born to them. The eldest, Vanessa (1879–1961; later, Bell) became an important avant-garde visual artist; the second, Thoby (1880–1906) died tragically young; and the youngest, Adrian (1883–1948), became a psychoanalyst and prominent pacifist. Virginia's (secular) godfather was the distinguished American poet and critic James Russell Lowell (1819–91), whom Leslie Stephen met in America, and who became ambassador to the Court of St James in the 1880s, during which time he became an intimate of the Stephen household. Indeed, many of the period's most notable intellectuals, artists and writers were visitors to the Stephen household.

That household, in 22 Hyde Park Gate, London (formerly the Duckworth home), crammed into its narrow and gloomy confines, then, numerous children and several servants. But it transferred every summer, for the first ten years of Woolf's childhood, to Talland House, Cornwall, the scene of her childhood idylls. It was in this house that she enjoyed her formative, blissful, experience of hearing waves and a window blind moving. These childhood summers 'permeated' her life, she claims, 'how much so I could never explain' (*D2* 103). In both locations the Stephen household was dominated by the scholarly and critical activities of Leslie Stephen. Woolf drew on her memories of her holidays in Cornwall for *To the Lighthouse*, which was conceived in part as an elegy on her parents. Her father was a vigorous walker and an Alpinist of some renown, a member of the Alpine Club and editor of the *Alpine Journal* from 1868 to 1872; he was the first person to climb the Schreckhorn in the Alps and he wrote on Alpine pleasures in *The Playground of Europe* (1871). By the time he married Julia Duckworth in 1878, however, a more sedentary Leslie Stephen was the established editor of the *Cornhill Magazine*, from which he later resigned to take up the editorship of the *Dictionary of National Biography* in 1882, the year of Woolf's birth. Stephen laboured on this monumental Victorian enterprise until 1990, editing single-handed the first twenty-six volumes and writing well over 300 biographical entries. He also published numerous volumes of criticism, the most important of which were on eighteenth-century thought and literature.

Meanwhile, the Stephen children enjoyed inventing nightly stories between themselves and also produced a weekly paper, *The Hyde Park Gate News*, for the entertainment of their parents.[2] Woolf recalls awaiting her mother's response:

> How excited I used to be when 'The Hyde Park Gate News' was laid on her plate on Monday morning, and she liked something I had written! Never shall I forget my extremity of pleasure – it was like being a violin and being played upon – when I found that she had sent a story of mine to Madge Symonds; it was so imaginative, she said; it was about souls flying round and choosing bodies to be born into. (*MOB* 95)

But there were darker undercurrents in this idyllic life. In 1891 Laura (1870–1945), Woolf's half-sister from her father's first marriage, was considered slow and disturbed enough to merit permanent consignment to an asylum. Woolf's childhood and adolescence were marred by sexual abuse at the hands of her half-brothers from her mother's first marriage, especially George, a matter of incendiary concern for some biographers. Vanessa, Thoby, Virginia and Adrian, however, enjoyed among themselves a close-knit and happy childhood. Virginia and Vanessa were not schooled like their brothers, but educated at home. Both parents contributed to Virginia's education, but it was her father who shaped her intellectual foundations, encouraging her to roam freely, from an early age, through his extensive library, and later giving her daily supervision in reading, writing and translation (of Greek and Latin).

It was her mother, however, who was, as Woolf later recalled, 'in the very centre of that great Cathedral space which was childhood . . . the creator of that crowded merry world . . . there it always was, the common life of the family, very merry, very stirring, crowded with people; and she was the centre' (*MOB* 75). Julia Stephen did not seem to exist as a separate person in her own right, but rather she became the personification of the Stephen household life. 'She was the whole thing; Talland House was full of her; Hyde Park Gate was full of her,' Woolf later recalled, realising that this 'general' existence explained 'why it was that it was impossible for her to leave a very private and particular impression upon a child. She was keeping what I call in my shorthand the panoply of life – that which we all lived in common — in being' (*MOB*). When her mother died in May 1895, Virginia, at the age of thirteen, suffered her first breakdown, and the family endured a deeply unhappy period of mourning. After this tragic loss, Leslie Stephen embarked on the compilation of a family memoir of Julia, which became known as the 'Mausoleum Book'. The brunt of Leslie Stephen's gloomy domestic demands, and of his need for solace, was born by Stella, his step-daughter, who also became a much-appreciated maternal figure to the Stephen children. 'It was Stella who lifted the canopy again,' Woolf recalls: 'A little light crept in' (*MOB* 95).

It was in January 1897 that she began her first diary. The entry for 24 February begins typically: 'Nessa went to her drawing. Father and I went out for our walk after breakfast.'[3] Vanessa went to art classes while Virginia was tutored by their father. She records a daily life packed with reading under her father's guidance, his tuition often preceded by a morning walk together; and she gives lively accounts of excursions into London on shopping errands, charitable visits and social calls; also of various private lessons, of her father's reading Walter Scott, William Wordsworth and many other writers to them, and of Stella's companionship and administration of household affairs. It was difficult for Stella to extricate herself from her stepfather's household when she married Jack Hills in April 1897, and after her marriage she lived with her husband in a house in the same street so as to continue with her attentions. But this happy interlude was cut short by her sudden death, while pregnant, in July 1897. This second loss was devastating: 'the blow, the second blow of death, struck on me; tremulous, filmy eyed as I was, with my wings still creased, sitting there on the edge of my broken chrysalis' (*MOB* 124). Her journal entries for the hot summer that followed are brief and telegraphic, but as well as the gloom and emotional turbulence of grief, they record the Stephen family pleasures of reading, playing cricket and moth-hunting.

After Stella's death, Leslie Stephen 'was quite prepared to take Vanessa for his next victim', as Virginia recalls in her 1904 memoir of her sister. Vanessa took the brunt of their father's monstrous and gloomy rages with memorable stoicism: 'she stood before him like a stone' (*MOB* 64). His children took him to be 'a tyrant of inconceivable selfishness, who had replaced the beauty and merriment of the dead with ugliness and gloom' (*MOB* 65). Woolf concedes that 'we were bitter, harsh and to a great extent, unjust', but that nevertheless 'even now it seems to me that there was some truth in our complaint' (*MOB* 65). Later, as well as the 'tyrant father', Woolf was able to recall with some readerly, if not filial, affection the 'writer father', and she records his continuing influence on her reading: 'I always read *Hours in a Library* by way of filling out my ideas . . . and always find something to fill out; to correct; to stiffen my fluid vision.' Reading her father's published works, she finds not a 'subtle' nor an 'imaginative mind' but a 'strong' and 'conventional' one: 'I get a sense of Leslie Stephen, the muscular agnostic; cheery, hearty; always cracking up sense and manliness; and crying down sentiment and vagueness' (*MOB* 127). It is important to recognise Woolf's acknowledgement of her father's dually formative influence. The domestic dictator was also an intellectual who powerfully shaped her developing intellect, even if, at times, antithetically so: 'just as a dog takes a bite of grass, I take a bite of him medicinally' (*MOB* 128).

By the close of the nineteenth century her studies with her father were being supplemented by tuition in the classics from Dr Warr of King's College, Kensington, and from Clara Pater, sister of the English essayist and critic Walter Pater (1839–94). Woolf was very fond of Clara and an exchange between them later became the basis for her short story 'Moments of Being: Slater's Pins Have No Points' (1928). Thoby boarded at Clifton College, Bristol, Adrian was a dayboy at Westminster School, and Vanessa attended Cope's School of Art. Thoby, and later Adrian, eventually went to Trinity College, Cambridge, and Vanessa undertook training in the visual arts (attending the Slade School of Fine Art for a while). From 1902 Virginia's tuition in classics passed from Clara Pater to the very capable Janet Case, one of the first graduates from Girton College, Cambridge, and a committed feminist. The sisters visited Cambridge a number of times to meet Thoby, whose friends there included Clive Bell (1881–1964), Lytton Strachey (1880–1932), Leonard Woolf (1880–1969) and Saxon Sydney-Turner.

Leslie Stephen died in 1904. In that year his children retreated to Wales for a period and then travelled in Italy. Vanessa and Virginia went on to Paris, where they met up with Clive Bell. On returning to London, Virginia suffered a severe, suicidal breakdown. But several positive changes also occurred. During her sister's convalescence Vanessa moved the Stephen household to 46 Gordon Square, Bloomsbury, a move that ushered in a new period of freedom and independence, particularly for the sisters. They relished creating a new domestic interior that replaced the dark and intricately patterned Morris wallpapers of Hyde Park Gate's gloomy confines with 'washes of plain distemper' and fresh white and green chintzes. Domestic practices were revolutionised, too. Woolf recalls, in her memoir of 'Old Bloomsbury' (*c.*1922), their creation of an environment in which to paint and to write rather than to worry about bourgeois tea-table conventions: 'Everything was going to be new; everything was going to be different. Everything was on trial' (*MOB* 201).

In that same year she assisted F. W. Maitland with a biography of her father, and her first (anonymous) review appeared in the *Guardian*. In 1905 she began work as a teacher of literature at Morley College in South London, and travelled to Portugal. Thoby began hosting 'Thursday Evenings' in the Bloomsbury house, and Vanessa founded the Friday Club, a society in which young, and at first, female, artists could meet, debate and exhibit work. As well as Virginia, Vanessa and Adrian, in the years that followed core Bloomsbury members were to include the high-ranking civil servant Saxon Sydney-Turner, the critic Lytton Strachey, the art critics Roger Fry (1866–1934) and Clive Bell, Desmond (1877–1952) and Molly MacCarthy, the artist Duncan Grant (1885–1978), the economist John Maynard Keynes (1883–1946), the novelist E. M. Forster (1879–1970) and the political journalist and publisher Leonard Woolf, plus James and Alix Strachey, Marjorie Strachey, Karin Stephen (Adrian's wife), and the society hostess Lady Ottoline Morrell.

The Bloomsbury Group has been characterised as a liberal, pacifist, and at times libertine, intellectual enclave of Cambridge-based privilege. The Cambridge men of the group (Bell, Forster, Fry, Keynes, Strachey, Sydney-Turner) were members of the elite and secret society of Cambridge Apostles. Woolf's aesthetic understanding, and broader philosophy, were in part shaped by, and at first primarily interpreted in terms of, (male) Bloomsbury's dominant aesthetic and philosophical preoccupations, rooted in the work of G. E. Moore (a central influence on the Apostles), and culminating in Fry's and Clive Bell's differing brands of pioneering aesthetic formalism. 'The main things which Moore instilled deep into our minds and characters,' Leonard Woolf recalls, 'were his peculiar passion for truth, for clarity and common sense, and a passionate belief in certain values.'[4] Increasing awareness of Woolf's feminism, however, and of the influence on her work of other women artists, writers and thinkers has meant that these Moorean and male points of reference, though of importance, are no longer considered adequate in approaching Woolf's work, and her intellectual development under the tutelage of women, together with her involvement with feminist thinkers and activists, is also now acknowledged.

After an ill-fated family visit to Greece in 1906, Thoby died of typhoid, at the age of twenty-six. Vanessa married Clive Bell in 1907. Leaving the newly-weds to Gordon Square, Virginia moved with Adrian to 29 Fitzroy Square, where they continued hosting 'Thursday Evenings'. She presided as hostess over meetings that were as often bawdy and childish as erudite and intellectually rarefied. 'If you could say what you liked about art, sex or religion,' her sister recalls, 'you could also talk freely and very likely dully about the ordinary doings of daily life.'[5] Bloomsbury life was defined by the freedom to talk, without self-consciousness, about anything at all, a reaction in part to the 'darkness and silence' of Hyde Park Gate where communication was often strained, and the overbearing Leslie Stephen 'could only be spoken to through a tube and if it was shy work doing this in front of the family,' Vanessa recalls, 'it was worse with strangers there. Then his sighs and groans needed accounting for . . . and even when accounted for did not lead to cheerfulness.'[6] Compare and contrast this scene with the infamous moment, in Fitzroy Square, when Lytton Strachey, 'point[ing] his finger at a stain on Vanessa's white dress', enquired: 'Semen?' And 'with that one word', Woolf recalls, 'all the barriers of reticence and reserve went down. A flood of the sacred fluid seemed to overwhelm us. Sex permeated our conversation. The word bugger was never far from our lips' (*MOB* 213). The licentious behaviour of Vanessa and Maynard Keynes together on a settee became the stuff of Bloomsbury legend, too. Virginia and Adrian began to have German lessons in Fitzroy Square, and it was there that in 1907, Woolf began to write 'Melymbrosia', her first novel, which was later published as *The Voyage Out* (1915).

If the word 'bugger' and her male homosexual friends seemed to dominate the conversation of Woolf's circle, it is also the case that she was building a reputation for herself as an incorrigible flirt with other women. 'I am so susceptible to female charms,' she wrote to Violet Dickinson in 1903, 'in fact I offered my blistered heart to one in Paris, if not two' (*L1* 69–70). Dickinson, initially a friend of Stella Duckworth's, became very close to Woolf, who wrote to her in an erotic vein of the 'astonishing . . . depths – hot volcano depths – your finger has stirred in Sparroy – hitherto entirely quiescent' (*L1* 85). She presented Dickinson with a mock biography of Dickinson and her close friend Lady Robert ('Nellie') Cecil, 'Friendships Gallery' (1907), which she typed in violet ink and bound in violet leather.[7] Vanessa remarked, in

1906, on her sister's liability to 'get up a flirtation in the train. You really aren't safe to be trusted alone. I know some lady will get a written promise of marriage out of you soon and then where will you be?' (*VBL* 37).

In 1908 Vanessa's first child, Julian was born. This event inspired Virginia to write a memoir of her sister for her nephew, which included portraits of their mother Julia, and half-sister Stella, too. But this was also a time when Vanessa's husband Clive began intimate flirtations with her sister. Virginia seems to have enjoyed and encouraged this intimacy, which fell short of sexual consummation and comprised intellectual as well as emotional bonds. It caused friction between the sisters, yet they remained close. 'Whisper into your wife's ear', Virginia wrote to Bell in August 1908, 'that I love her. I expect she will scold you for tickling her (when she hears the message)' (*L1* 362). Vanessa was Woolf's declared inspiration for characters in *The Voyage Out*, *Night and Day* (1919) and *To the Lighthouse* (1927). Clive Bell read and commented on early drafts of Woolf's first novel, and she valued his literary mentorship. He combined genuine encouragement with constructive criticism. He recognised her words to have the 'force' of poetry, and the work to be 'alive' and 'subtle', but he also counselled against passages that were 'too didactic, not to say priggish'. He identified her tendency in draft to draw 'marked contrasts between the subtle, sensitive, tactful, gracious, delicately perceptive, & perspicacious women, & the obtuse, vulgar, blind, florid, rude, tactless, emphatic, indelicate, vain, tyrannical, stupid men, [a]s not only rather absurd, but rather bad art' (*VWB2* 209–10). Woolf later acknowledged to him that he was 'the first person who ever thought I'd write well' (*VWB2* 212).

In the spring of 1908 Virginia holidayed in St Ives, where she was joined by the Bells, and she accompanied them in the autumn to Italy, then Paris. During this period she refused romantic attention and proposals of marriage from a number of young men associated with her brother's Cambridge circle – Edward Hilton Young, Walter Lamb and Sydney Waterlow.[8] She seemed to prefer the security of flirtations, it has been suggested, with men, such as her brother-in-law, whom she could not possibly marry. In February 1909 she was even engaged very briefly to Lytton Strachey, an open homosexual with whom she enjoyed an intimate and flirtatious intellectual friendship.

It is significant that Strachey recounted their twenty-four-hour engagement in letters to his friend Leonard Woolf, who was at that time on colonial service in Ceylon. Indeed, his account 'was written *in reply* to Leonard's own fantasy of marriage to her' (*VWL* 261). He confesses to Leonard that even as he proposed, he saw 'it would be death if she accepted', and that the next day she 'declared she was not in love with me, and I observed finally that

I would not marry her. So things have simply reverted' (*LWL* 147). Virginia Woolf later referred to Lytton as 'perfect as friend, only he's a female friend' (*L1* 492). In the same letter in which he recounts the aborted engagement, Strachey encourages Woolf himself to become Virginia's suitor: 'You *would* be great enough and you'll have the immense advantage of physical desire.' This recommendation, to give something of the fuller flavour of their exchange, is followed by an aside on an erotic poem sent to him by Leonard: 'your poem disproves your theory. Imaginations are nothing; facts are all. A penis actually erected – on becoming erect – is cataclysmal. In imagination it's a mere shade. That, in my view, is the point of art, which converts imaginations into actualities.' In the following months Strachey continued to press the case with his friend: 'Do try it. She's an astounding woman, and I'm the only man in the universe who would have refused her; even I sometimes have my doubts. You might, of course, propose by telegram, and she'ld probably accept.' By August 1909 he writes: 'Your destiny is clearly marked out for you . . . You must marry Virginia . . . She's the only woman in the world with sufficient brains; it's a miracle that she should exist. . . . She's young, wild, inquisitive, discontented, and longing to be in love. If I were you I should telegraph' (*LWL* 147, 148–9). And in September 1909 Leonard responds: 'Of course I know that the one thing to do would be to marry Virginia. I am only frightened that when I come back in Dec 1910 I may' (*LWL* 149–50).

Meanwhile, Virginia started working for women's suffrage. She also became better acquainted with Ottoline Morrell. In April 1909 her aunt Caroline Emelia Stephen died and left her a legacy of £2,500. She travelled to Florence that year with Vanessa and Clive Bell, and to Bayreuth for the Wagner festival, and then visited Dresden with her brother Adrian and Sydney-Turner. On Christmas Eve 1909 she had a sudden impulse to go to Cornwall, and she spent the festive period alone there, tramping and reading.

The 1910s

1910 was a significant year for Woolf and Bloomsbury. she later marked it out as a year of cataclysmic change, in her essay 'Mr Bennett and Mrs Brown' (1924), and developments in her personal life, as well as in the public profile of the Bloomsbury Group, occurred in a broader context of social and political upheaval. In 1910 she 'was involved in three events', her biographer Hermione Lee observes, 'which came to be read as connected expressions of British subversiveness: the suffrage movement, the *Dreadnought* Hoax, and the Post-Impressionist exhibition' (*VWL* 279).

Janet Case encouraged Virginia to become more active in the suffrage movement as their campaigns stepped up the pressure in anticipation of the general election, and she found herself, early in 1910, among 'ardent but educated young women' addressing envelopes (*L1* 422). In February she took part in the notorious *Dreadnought* Hoax. Virginia and her brother Adrian, Duncan Grant, Horace Cole and others, masquerading as the Emperor of Abyssinia and entourage, conned their way past naval high security into a guided tour of the warship HMS *Dreadnought*. Roger Fry was introduced to Bloomsbury by Clive Bell, and he spoke to the Friday Club not long after the hoax. During the summer of 1910 Virginia's mental health declined and during July and August she took a rest cure at a private nursing home in Twickenham, which she periodically attended between 1910 and 1915 on the advice of Dr George Savage, the Stephen family doctor and eminent neurologist who treated her until 1913. After this first stay she went on a walking tour in Cornwall with Jean Thomas, the devout Christian proprietor of the nursing home. In August the Bells' second son, Quentin, was born. Virginia joined them at Studland, Dorset, before settling back to life in London in the autumn.

Bloomsbury notoriety was compounded in November 1910 with the opening of Fry's groundbreaking exhibition 'Manet and the Post-Impressionists', the first major showing in Britain of the work of Van Gogh, Gauguin, Cézanne and other avant-garde continental artists. It met with huge public and critical outrage. Virginia and Vanessa scandalously masqueraded as nearly nude 'Gauguin girls' at the Post-Impressionist Ball. Within days of the Post-Impressionist exhibition opening at the Grafton Galleries, Virginia attended the mass rally of suffragists at the Albert Hall on 12 November 1910, which struck her as dull and ineffectual, the speakers' voices 'like the tollings of a bell'. During this period she records that her 'time has been wasted a good deal upon Suffrage' (*L1* 438). She was not present, though, among the hundreds of suffragette demonstrators assaulted and imprisoned on 'Black Friday' on 18 November, an event that ushered in the era of suffragette violence, 'a programme of window-smashing, picture-slashing, arson and bombs',[9] but she cannot have escaped the reporting of this momentous day alongside the reviews of the already notorious Post-Impressionist exhibition. Feminist activism interpenetrated with avant-garde art.

Suffragist politics were influential, in any case, in Bloomsbury: Marjorie Strachey was a suffragette, and Pernel, Pippa, and Ray Strachey were suffragists; the Bloomsbury artist Duncan Grant had won a suffragist poster prize in 1909. Virginia evokes the frisson of being at the heart of such matters with a touch of acid coolness when she writes to her friend Violet Dickinson:

> I suppose you have been going everywhere – to the Grafton Galleries,
> and the Bernard Shaw play [*Misalliance*]. Now that Clive is in the van
> of aesthetic opinion, I hear a great deal about pictures. I dont think
> them so good as books. But why all the Duchesses are insulted by the
> post-impressionists, a modest sample set of painters, innocent even
> of indecency, I cant conceive. However, one mustn't say that they are
> like other pictures, only better, because that makes everyone
> angry.   (*L1* 440)

Modern women, it appears to her, take Shaw's socialist-feminist plays and Bell's avant-garde art in their stride.

In late December 1910 she found a place to rent in Firle, Sussex, and in January 1911 she took possession of Little Talland House, which she visited many times over the year, to write her novel *The Voyage Out* and entertain various friends and family. In the spring she made a rescue visit to Vanessa in Turkey, where she had suffered a miscarriage while travelling with Clive and Roger Fry. It was at this time that Vanessa began her affair with Fry. They all returned to London in April on the Orient Express. During this period Virginia saw much of Ka Cox and the circle of 'Neo-Pagans' who worshipped nature, swimming naked and sleeping out in the open, and in the summer she went camping in Devon with Cox, Maynard Keynes and Rupert Brooke, among others. She also spent a number of days with Brooke at The Old Vicarage, Grantchester, where they swam in the nude together. In July 1911 Leonard Woolf, recently returned from Ceylon, dined with the Bells at Gordon Square. Virginia joined the party after dinner. Leonard, finding 'almost the only things which had not changed [to be] the furniture and extraordinary beauty of the two Miss Stephens', was impressed by the 'greater intimacy and freedom', intellectual and sexual, than he had found in the circle seven years previously; and that these freedoms had been markedly embraced by the women: 'complete freedom of thought and speech was now extended to Vanessa and Virginia, Pippa and Marjorie'.[10]

In December 1911 Virginia and Adrian moved to 38 Brunswick Square along with Maynard Keynes, Duncan Grant and Leonard Woolf. Virginia also negotiated to rent Asheham House, in Beddingham, Sussex. In January 1912 Leonard proposed marriage. She was unable to answer directly and he pressed further in a passionate letter: 'It isn't, really it isnt, merely because you are so beautiful – though of course that is a large reason & so it should be – that I love you: it is your mind & your character – I have never known anyone like you in that – wont you believe me?' (*VWB1* 181). Virginia asked for time, to 'go on as before', and to be left free (*VWB1* 181). Shortly afterwards she suffered a relapse of mental illness and returned for a while to

Jean Thomas's nursing home. Leonard's resignation was accepted by the Colonial Office on 7 May, and on 29 May Virginia agreed to marry him.

Leonard Woolf was two years older than Virginia, whom he had first met in 1901 in the rooms of her brother Thoby at Cambridge. He went from St Paul's School to Trinity College on a scholarship in 1899 and was the first Jew to be elected to the Cambridge Apostles. His father Sidney Woolf (1844–92) was a barrister who died prematurely, leaving his widow, Marie, with the care of their ten children. After Cambridge, Leonard reluctantly entered the Colonial Civil Service and he served in Ceylon for seven years. The experience forged him as a passionate anti-imperialist. In 1911 he began writing a novel based on his experiences, but written from the point of view of the Sinhalese; *The Village in the Jungle* was published in 1913. This work may have influenced his wife's novel *The Voyage Out*, which has a fictional colonial setting. On his return to England he became a committed socialist and he was active on the left for most of his life, publishing numerous pamphlets and books of significance on national and inter-national politics. His role as intimate literary mentor to Virginia Woolf has sometimes overshadowed his considerable import as a political writer in his own right.

Leonard and Virginia married in August 1912. Virginia was 30. Soon after her marriage she suffered another breakdown and her mental health declined sporadically over the following year, culminating in a suicide at-tempt in September 1913. They were advised against having children because of Virginia's recurring depressive illness, a cause of some regret to her, and a point of much heated debate among her later biographers. Her suicidal phase came shortly after the acceptance for publication in 1913 of her first novel, *The Voyage Out*, which was published in 1915 by her half-brother Gerald Duckworth. In the autumn of 1912, Vanessa Bell and Duncan Grant were among those representing the English artists converted to the new avant-garde aesthetic, in the Second Post-Impressionist exhibition. They were co-directors of the Omega Workshops, founded by Fry in July 1913, which were established to employ young artists, on a strictly part-time basis, to design and make a wide range of objects, trinkets, textiles and furniture. Bloomsbury domestic interiors and clothes, including Woolf's, were fash-ioned in the distinctive Omega style. Other Omega artists included Nina Hamnett and the Vorticist Wyndham Lewis, who fell out with the Blooms-bury faction of Omega over their commission for the Ideal Home exhibition of 1913. From then on a sworn enemy of Bloomsbury, Lewis later savaged its members, including Woolf, in his satires of the 1930s, *The Apes of God* (1930) and *Men Without Art* (1934).

Vanessa Bell's design work for Omega propelled her into making some of the earliest, and finest, examples of abstract art, such as her colourist painting of 1914, entitled *Abstract*, now in the Tate Gallery, London. Leonard Woolf was secretary to the 1912 exhibition; its catalogue included Fry's exposition of the new formalism and Clive Bell's highly influential formulation of 'Significant Form', a theory he expanded for his bestselling book *Art* (1914). Bloomsbury formalism is encapsulated here as the 'aesthetic rapture' brought on by the 'combination of lines and colours'. Lily Briscoe, the artist in Woolf's novel *To the Lighthouse*, appears to be a disciple of this aesthetic formalism, if not a fictional portrait of Vanessa Bell herself, when she represents the classical figures of mother and child as a purple triangle. Woolf also conceived the 'chilly' Katharine Hilbery, heroine of *Night and Day*, as a partial portrait of her sister Vanessa 'concealing her passion for painting and forced to go into society by George [Duckworth]' (*L2* 400).

After his involvement with the Second Post-Impressionist exhibition, however, Leonard Woolf's career did not proceed in arts administration; he followed a more political path. Between his wife's bouts of depression in 1913 they toured the cities of northern England together pursuing Leonard's study of the Co-Operative movement, and in June they attended the Women's Co-Operative Congress in Newcastle upon Tyne with Margaret Llewellyn-Davies. They also met and befriended the Fabian socialists Sydney and Beatrice Webb. In 1914 Vanessa left her husband Clive Bell for Duncan Grant, an open homosexual who had had an affair and lived with her brother Adrian. It was after Adrian's marriage to Karin Costelloe that Grant turned to Vanessa, but he also began an affair with David Garnett. The three lived together on a farm in Sussex during the early part of the First World War, the two men having declared themselves, along with Lytton Strachey, conscientious objectors (Leonard Woolf was rejected for military service in 1916 on the medical grounds of his permanent tremor). In 1916 Bell, Grant and Garnett found and moved to Charleston, the Sussex house that became Vanessa's and Grant's permanent home. Meanwhile, the Woolfs had moved to Hogarth House in Richmond in 1915, and there, with a handpress on the dining-room table, they launched the Hogarth Press in 1917. Their first publication was *Two Stories* (1917) by Leonard and Virginia Woolf ('Three Jews' and 'The Mark on the Wall', respectively). Woolf suffered severe bouts of mental illness after the publication of *The Voyage Out* in March 1915.

Woolf met Dora Carrington, the artist and devoted companion to Lytton Strachey, in 1916 when Carrington was obliged to explain to her the circumstances in which she, David Garnett and Barbara Bagenal had forced entry into Asheham House and spent the night there. Around 1917 Woolf met Katherine Mansfield and the Hogarth Press published Mansfield's *Prelude* in 1918. According to Woolf's diary, her first impression, at a dinner in October of that year, was that Mansfield 'stinks . . . like a civet cat that had taken to street walking. In truth, I'm a little shocked by her commonness at first sight; lines so hard & cheap. However, when this diminishes, she is so intelligent & inscrutable that she repays friendship.' In the same entry Woolf records finding her 'illuminating' on Henry James (*D1* 58). Woolf's admiration of Mansfield was poisoned by her sense of rivalry, and she understood their friendship to be 'almost entirely founded on quicksands' (*D1* 243), but when Mansfield died in 1922 Woolf saw 'no point in writing. Katherine won't read it' (*D2* 226), and recognised a commonality she would 'never find with anyone else' (*D2* 227).

In 1918 Angelica Bell was born, the daughter of Vanessa and Duncan Grant. During this period Woolf attended the 1917 Club, a left-wing political society founded by Leonard, and was organiser of her local Women's Co-Operative Guild at Richmond. Her experimental story 'Kew Gardens' was published by Hogarth in 1919, and her second novel, *Night and Day*, was published by Duckworth. Woolf was hurt by Mansfield's review of this novel as out of touch with modern methods and modern life. After *Night and Day* the Hogarth Press published all Woolf's major works. The *Times Literary Supplement* published her influential essay 'Modern Novels' (1919), which was revised for publication by Hogarth as 'Modern Fiction' in *The Common Reader* (1925). Harriet Weaver approached the Woolfs with a manuscript of James Joyce's *Ulysses* in April 1918, but they were unable to 'tackle' a work of that size (*D1* 136), and Woolf's account of their meeting suggests other kinds of strain, too, brought on by the nature of the work and its agent:

> Her neat mauve suit fitted both soul & body; her grey gloves laid straight by her plate symbolised domestic rectitude; her table manners were those of a well bred hen. We could get no talk to go. Possibly the poor woman was impeded by her sense that what she had in the brownpaper parcel was quite out of keeping with her own contents. But then how did she ever come in contact with Joyce & the rest? Why does their filth seek exit from her mouth? Heaven knows. . . . We both looked at the MS. which seems to be an attempt to push the bounds of expression further on, but still all in the same direction.   (*D1* 140)

Her private misgivings about Joyce aside, her essay 'Modern Novels', published a year later, marked her as one of his earliest defenders in print.

Having been given notice to quit Asheham House, in 1919 the Woolfs bought Monk's House in Rodmell, Sussex, 'an unpretending house . . . of many doors' (*D1* 286) with a garden that became Leonard's passion. It became their retreat from London; they spent nearly every summer there until Woolf's death in 1941.

The 1920s

In March 1920 the first meeting of the Memoir Club was held, its members being the thirteen original members of the Bloomsbury Group, who later came to be known among themselves as 'Old Bloomsbury': Vanessa and Clive Bell, Virginia and Leonard Woolf, Desmond and Molly MacCarthy, Lytton Strachey, Adrian Stephen, John Maynard Keynes, E. M. Forster, Roger Fry, Duncan Grant and Saxon Sydney-Turner. The club's founding principle was 'absolute frankness', and the members met to dine and read memoirs to each other. Woolf's first set of experimental short stories, *Monday or Tuesday*, was published by Hogarth in 1921, followed by the novel *Jacob's Room* in 1922. Woolf's control over the production of her own work is a significant factor in her genesis as a writer. The Hogarth Press became an important and influential publishing house in the decades that followed. It was responsible, for example, for the first major works of Freud in English, beginning in 1922, and published significant works by key modernist writers such as T. S. Eliot and Gertrude Stein. Woolf herself set the type for the Hogarth edition of Eliot's *The Waste Land* (1923), which he read to them in June 1922, and which she found to have 'great beauty & force of phrase: symmetry; & tensity. What connects it together, I'm not so sure' (*D2* 178). In 1922 Woolf met the writer Vita Sackville-West, who was to join Vanessa Bell and Leonard Woolf as the most significant people in her life. In 1924 the Woolfs left Hogarth House and moved (with the printing press) to 52 Tavistock Square. By the time *Jacob's Room* was published, Woolf's reputation as an avant-garde writer and important literary critic was consolidating. *Jacob's Room* was the first in a sequence of formally experimental, increasingly lyric, novels that would include *Mrs Dalloway* (1925), *To the Lighthouse* (1927), *Orlando: A Biography* (1928) and *The Waves* (1931). Woolf's highly influential modernist and feminist literary theories were expounded in 'Mr Bennett and Mrs Brown', and *A Room of One's Own* (1929), the tract based on her lectures on 'Women and Fiction' at Newnham and Girton Colleges, Cambridge. She also published two collections of essays, *The Common Reader* and *The Common Reader; Second Series* (1932). She was awarded the 1927–28

Prix Femina for *To the Lighthouse*. This was a period of increasing commercial success for Woolf in which she took great pride as both writer and publisher.

Vanessa Bell's collaboration with her sister was vital in these years. From *Jacob's Room* on, her art work became integral to the cover designs on all Woolf's books, with the exception of *Orlando* and *Flush* (1933), the latter nevertheless including four illustrations by her. She illustrated Woolf's *Kew Gardens* (1919), and *Monday or Tuesday* (1921), and designed the wolf's head colophon of the Hogarth Press. Although her husband was often her highly valued and respected first reader of work in draft, Woolf considered her sister to be her primary audience: 'I always feel I'm writing more for you than for anybody' (*L4* 390). Later, in the early 1930s, Woolf wrote the forewords to catalogues for two of her sister's exhibitions of paintings, which celebrate Bell's artistic virtuosity. There are more overt tributes to her aesthetic influence at work all through Woolf's writing. 'Are not all Arts her tributaries, all sciences her continents and the globe itself but a painted ball in the enclosure of her arms? But you dwell in the Temple,' the young Woolf had written to Clive Bell, 'and I am a worshipper without' (*L1* 282). Woolf's adoration for her sister-muse endured long after her brother-in-law fell from favour and it was the foundation of their extraordinary professional collaboration.

In 1925 the Hogarth Press published Jane Harrison's *Reminiscences of a Student's Life*. Harrison (1850–1928), the noted Cambridge anthropologist and mythologist, was greatly admired by both Virginia and Leonard Woolf. While in Paris in 1923 Woolf spent a week largely in the company of Harrison and her partner Hope Mirrlees, who lived there and in London. 'This gallant old lady,' Woolf reports, 'took my fancy greatly; partly for her superb high thinking agnostic ways, partly for her appearance' (*L3* 58). They remained close friends, and Harrison has come to be acknowledged as a powerful intellectual influence on Woolf. Woolf records her frequent visits to the ailing Harrison, and, in a stunning diary entry, how Harrison's death was broken to her the following day by Mirrlees whom she met by chance walking in St George's Fields graveyard in Bloomsbury: 'we kissed by Cromwell's daughter's grave, where Shelley used to walk, for Jane's death' (*D3* 180). The funeral, however, left Woolf unmoved, for 'as usual the obstacle of not believing dulled & bothered' her, and she questioned the relevance of God and 'the Grace of Christ' for Harrison, too (*D3* 181).

In 1925 Woolf began an affair with Sackville-West, who was married to Harold Nicolson, the diplomat and writer, and the development of their close relationship, which does not seem to have undermined either woman's marriage, coincided with Woolf's most productive years as a writer. Sackville-West, the only child of the third Baron Sackville and Victoria Lady Sackville, was barred from inheriting the family house, Knole, in Kent, after a highly publicised lawsuit taken to court by her uncle in 1910 to establish his succession to the title. A prolific writer of poetry, fiction, biography and travel books, she was also a notable gardener. After their marriage she and her husband lived at Long Barn, near Knole, from 1915, then in 1930 they bought nearby Sissinghurst Castle, where Sackville-West's splendid garden is now maintained by the National Trust. Her notoriety has hardly faded since her infamous two-year affair with Violet Trefusis. The women's husbands flew to Paris to terminate their elopement in 1920, and Sackville-West returned to an open and happy marriage with Nicolson, who himself pursued homosexual extramarital affairs. They had two sons, Nigel and Benedict.

In June 1927 Woolf joined Leonard, Sackville-West, Nicolson and other friends on an expedition to Yorkshire, to witness (along with 20,000 others), the first total eclipse of the sun to be visible from Britain in several hundred years. It had a momentous influence on Woolf: she recorded it in her diary, drew upon it for her influential essay 'The Sun and the Fish' (1928), and rewrote it (in many drafts) for her closing meditation on 'the world seen without a self' in *The Waves* (pp. 310ff). Her novel *Orlando* celebrates and is dedicated to Sackville-West. Early in their affair Woolf describes Vita 'shin[ing] in the grocers shop in Sevenoaks with a candle lit radiance, stalking on legs like beech trees, pink glowing, grape clustered, pearl hung' (*D3* 52). At one point Vita wrote to her husband of her fear of 'arousing physical feelings in [Woolf], because of the madness',[11] but their relationship was nevertheless sexual and based on 'explicit acknowledgement of sexual attraction'.[12] But if she was seduced by Vita's long legs, and general aristocratic demeanour, Woolf did not appear to rate her writing, 'which she does with complete competency, and a pen of brass' (*L3* 150). Yet it would be a distortion of their relationship, as Suzanne Raitt has shown, to ignore Vita's writing as a significant factor in its dynamics.[13]

As Woolf was writing the last pages of *To the Lighthouse* in 1926, she experienced a deep sense of depression and recorded in her diary the aqueous vision of 'a fin passing far out' (*D3* 126). In May 1927 Vanessa wrote to her of the moths that flew around her house in Cassis on French summer evenings, and Woolf thought of 'nothing else but you and the moths for hours after' reading the letter (*L3* 372). Out of these two visionary moments was conceived 'The Moths', which became *The Waves*, Woolf's most acclaimed experimental, poetic novel. She spent the late 1920s rigorously pursuing and wrestling with her new creative form, 'this hideous shaping & moulding' (*D3* 301). As well as her visionary moments, Woolf experienced, in the same period, more granite-like ones. As she was writing 'Time Passes', the central section of *To the Lighthouse*, she was in London during the General Strike of May 1926. A supporter of the strike, with Leonard, she undertook to keep 'an exact diary of the Strike', and records:

> Everyone is bicycling; motor cars are huddled up with extra people. There are no buses. No placards. no newspapers. The men are at work in the road; water, gas & electricity are allowed; but at 11 the light was turned off. I sat in the press in the brown fog, while L. wrote an article for the Herald. A very revolutionary looking young man on a cycle arrived with the British Gazette. L. is to answer an article in this. All was military stern a little secret.   (*D3* 77)

In the summer of 1928, Woolf signed the petition in support of Radclyffe Hall's 'Sapphist' novel *The Well of Loneliness*, which had been published that year then banned for obscenity, and offered herself as a witness in its defence. In September she holidayed with Sackville-West for a week in Burgundy, France, from where Sackville-West wrote to her husband of how 'extraordinarily protective' she felt towards Woolf: 'The combination of that brilliant brain and fragile body is very lovable. She has a sweet childlike nature, from which her intellect is completely separate. I have never known anyone who was so profoundly sensitive, and who makes less of a business of that sensitiveness' (*L3* 533). Woolf, however, still missed her husband, to whom she wrote every day, signing off with one of her nicknames, 'Mandrill' (others include 'Goat' and 'the Apes'). While 'Vita is a perfect old hen' looking after her, 'Lord! how I adore you!,' she reassures Leonard, 'and you only think of me as a bagful of itching monkeys, and ship me to the Indies with indifference!' (*L3* 539). By the time Vita was discovering, in October 1928, a 'new form of Narcissism' by falling in love with Orlando (*L3* 574), her own fictional embodiment created by Woolf, their relationship off the page was beginning to cool. Later, in 1935, when the falling-off came, it came 'not with a quarrel, not with a bang, but as ripe fruit falls' (*D4* 287), and Woolf's loss of interest in her lover was confirmed by her sister's acid reports that Sackville-West 'has simply become Orlando the wrong way round – I mean turned into a man' (*VBL* 385). The new object of Sackville-West's desire by then was Gwen St Aubyn, her husband's sister. Woolf, meanwhile, came into the amorous sights of the feminist composer Ethel Smyth in the 1930s.

1930–1941

While Smyth eclipsed Sackville-West in Woolf's affections, her marriage to Leonard was as ever emotionally central, comfortable, and conducive to her creative productivity, as well as to her intellectual reflection and relaxation. She called him her 'inviolable centre' (*D5* 284). Her private writings indicate this sense of marital harmony and deep companionship. For example, a diary entry of November 1937 notes how 'the month has run through my fingers, with a walk or two: many letters & some divine quiet evenings. L. in his stall, I in mine, reading' (*D5* 120). The Woolfs travelled quite a lot in the 1930s. They holidayed in western France in 1931, drove through France and Italy in 1933, were in Ireland the following year, and in May 1935 undertook a European tour by car, spending a week in Holland and an unnerving three days in Nazi Germany, before meeting Vanessa, Quentin and Angelica Bell in Rome, and then returning home through France. They were in France again in 1937 and 1939. They broke the pattern and went north to Scotland and the Western Isles in the summer of 1938, and Woolf visited for the first and only time the Isle of Skye, where she had set *To the Lighthouse*. Not surprisingly for the daughter of an eighteenth-century specialist, she followed the itinerary of Dr Johnson's tour during her three days on the island, making endless pencil notes on the scenery and eavesdropping on conversations. She later regretted these 'Boswell experiments in Inns', when it came to writing them up for her diary (*D5* 154).

When Leonard, whom she considered her most 'honest' critic, read the manuscript of *The Waves* in 1931, he declared it 'a masterpiece' and 'the best of your books' (*D4* 35–6). While composing this, her most avant-garde, poetically stylised novel, Woolf also worked on her controversial essay 'Memories of a Working Women's Guild' (1930), which was commissioned by Margaret Llewellyn-Davies as an introduction to *Life As We Have Known It by Co-Operative Working Women*, published by Hogarth in 1931. Woolf wrote of her experience of working in the Women's Co-Operative Guild, and of her consciousness of how class issues affected her position there. As in other formative essays of this later period, such as 'The Leaning Tower' (1940), she ruminated on the prospects of the working classes producing a future great novelist or poet.

Woolf turned her back on a number of tokens of her rising eminence in the 1930s, including an offer of the Companion of Honour award, an invitation from Cambridge University to give the Clark lectures, and honorary doctorate degrees from Manchester University and Liverpool University. 'It is an utterly corrupt society,' she wrote in her diary, '. . . & I will take nothing that it can give me' (*D4* 147). In May 1931 she sat for the sculptor

Stephen Tomlin, whose bust of Woolf has been cast a number of times since. One bust stands in the garden of Monk's House, another in the National Gallery, and a third in Tavistock Square Gardens (the original plaster cast is at Charleston). But while she was sitting for this bust, ironically enough, she was reflecting, in an essay commissioned by *Good Housekeeping* magazine (1931), that 'the days of the small separate statue are over' (*LS* 70), and she looked forward to a more democratic form of commemoration.

When the poet John Lehmann went to work for the Hogarth Press, as an assistant and later co-director, he introduced the Woolfs to the younger wave of politically engaged writers, including W. H. Auden, Christopher Isherwood, Louis MacNeice, Cecil Day-Lewis and Stephen Spender. It was to Lehmann that Woolf addressed her 'Letter to a Young Poet' (1932), and they got on very well. His relationship with Leonard was prickly, however. At Ottoline Morrell's house Woolf met, in November 1934, a distinguished poet from the older generation and was in awe as she 'pressed his hand when we said goodbye with some emotion: thinking This is to press a famous hand', although she had met W. B. Yeats twenty odd years before. She describes him as 'a solid wedge of oak. His face is too fat; but it has its hatchet forehead in profile, under a tangle of grey & brown hair; the eyes are luminous, direct, but obscured under glasses; they have however seen close, the vigilant & yet wondering look of his early portraits.' Woolf found him discussing with Walter de la Mare 'dreaming states, & soul states; as others talk of Beaverbrook & free trade – as if matters of common knowledge. So familiar was he, that I perceived that he had worked out a complete psychology, which I could only catch on to momentarily in my alarming ignorance' (*D3* 329). In a similar encounter at Morrell's four years later, Woolf to her delight reports Yeats's commenting on *The Waves*: 'That comes after Stendhal he said. I see what you're at – But I want more humanity.' She records feeling 'Yeats' extreme directness, simplicity, & equality: liked his praise; liked him: but cant unriddle the universe at tea' (*D4* 255). For all her own visionary moments, Woolf treated Yeats's mysticism with the same atheistic scepticism that she reserved for more conventional religious belief.

When her young friend, and Hogarth Press author, Francis Birrell was dying, in the winter of 1934, of a brain tumour, Woolf was moved by his stoicism, calling him a 'credit to atheism' (*D4* 266). This decade was marked by grief at the deaths of others very close to Woolf, too. But it was also a period of sustained creativity, as well as of political struggle. In the 1930s Woolf supported her husband's increasing involvement with and work for the Labour Party, and her own work became more overtly political. Her antifascist activities included membership of a number of different organisations and committees, and Woolf's references to them in her letters and diaries have caused some confusion. Fortunately for Woolf readers, the literary historian, David Bradshaw has lucidly explained the precise nature of her involvement in these bodies.[14] Early in 1935 Woolf involved herself in preparations for an antifascist exhibition in London, and in November of that year the Cambridge Anti-Fascist exhibition, in Soho Square, duly documented the rising threat of fascism. Woolf expressed her concerns that the organising committee ignored 'the woman question' (*D4* 273). She also served on the committee organising the British delegation to the International Congress of Writers in Paris in June, 1935, but she did not attend in person despite E. M. Forster's attempts to persuade her. She did become involved in the subsequently established British Section of the International Association of Writers for the Defence of Culture (IAWDC), from which turbulent body she resigned in 1936, 'on the ground that my husband does all that for two or even one dozen' (*L6* 51).

The Woolfs were also involved, at the same time, with For Intellectual Liberty (FIL), which embraced a broader range of cultural activists against fascism, and included from its inception the Woolfs, Forster, Aldous Huxley and the sculptor Henry Moore. A meeting held at Adrian Stephen's home in November 1935 was attended by the Woolfs, Vanessa, Grant, Auden, Huxley, Moore, Herbert Read, C. P. Snow and others. This meeting struck Woolf 'dumb with helpless wonder' (*L5* 449). FIL was 'in time,' as Bradshaw shows, 'to become affiliated to the National Peace Council and the International Peace Campaign, and it would cooperate closely with the National Joint Committee for Spanish Relief . . . as well as with the China Campaign Committee, the Union of Democratic Control and the Artists International Association'.[15] Woolf's letters and diaries are full of committee fatigue, such as when she records that Leonard is 'doomed to another Committee' (*L5* 449), again designating him as the committee half of their partnership. She became increasingly exasperated by the IAWDC and the FIL, but 'her role as an FIL panellist and her vantage point as Leonard Woolf's partner meant that she still moved very much within that milieu'.[16] Bradshaw points out that Woolf distanced herself from ineffectual 'high-minded general appeals', and the bluster about intellectual freedom emanating from these male-dominated bodies, but was 'willing to respond to specific cases of injustice . . . and specific acts of fascist aggression, like the German re-occupation of the Rhineland'.[17] She was in effect adopting the outsider status she was to define for feminists in *Three Guineas* (1938).

The (draft) essay-novel *The Pargiters* (published posthumously in 1978), was an ambitious project conceived to combine critical and political argument with fictional narrative, which Woolf eventually divided for publication into two works, the epistolary antifascist, pacifist polemic, *Three Guineas* and the more conventional novel *The Years* (1937). Woolf's experiments in biography continued with *Flush: A Biography* (1933), a fictional and satirical portrait of the poet Elizabeth Barrett-Browning's spaniel, and with the more serious, straightforward (and for Woolf more difficult to write) biography, *Roger Fry* (1940). Bloomsbury lost Fry, in 1934, and Lytton Strachey before him, in January 1932, to early deaths. The loss of Strachey was compounded by Carrington's suicide just two months after, in March. Another old friend, Ka Cox, died of a heart attack in 1938. But the death, in 1937, of Woolf's nephew Julian, in the Spanish Civil War, was perhaps the bitterest blow. Vanessa found her sister her only comfort: 'I couldn't get on at all if it weren't for you' (*VWB2* 203). Julian, a radical thinker and aspiring writer, campaigned all his life against war, but he had to be dissuaded by his family from joining the International Brigade to fight Franco. Instead he worked as an ambulance driver, a role that did not prevent his death from shrapnel wounds. Woolf's *Three Guineas*, she wrote to his mother, was written 'as an argument with him' (*L6* 159).

In 1939 the Woolfs left Tavistock Square for 37 Mecklenburgh Square, and Woolf began writing 'A Sketch of the Past'. In the same year they met Sigmund Freud, who had arrived in London a refugee from the Nazis. When he came to tea this 'old fire now flickering' presented Woolf with a narcissus (*D5* 202). The Woolfs took refuge at Monk's House when the bombs started falling on London at the start of the Second World War. Mecklenburgh Square was bombed in 1940 but Woolf was able to salvage her diaries from the wreckage. She urged 'mental fight' against Hitlerism in a poignant late essay, 'Thoughts on Peace in an Air Raid' (1940), constructed in response to the sound of German bombers as they passed overhead, a sound that hovers, too, over her last entries in her unfinished memoir, 'A Sketch of the Past', written with a weather eye on 'invasions' and 'raids' (*MOB* 139). At the same time, she was in the process of finalising *Between the Acts*, her last novel, known in draft as *Pointz Hall*.

The circumstances of Woolf's suicide, and even the wording of her suicide notes, have been the object of considerable scholarly and popular interest and debate, which Chapter Two will briefly explore. But this chapter attempts to close in simple granite by recording that on 28 March 1941, fearing a return of her insanity at this dark pass in the war, Virginia Woolf committed suicide by drowning herself in the River Ouse. *Between the Acts* was published posthumously in July 1941.

Contexts

The prospect of accounting for the many contexts relevant to reading Virginia Woolf brings to mind her famous simile, in 'Kew Gardens' (1919), for the city of London: 'a vast nest of Chinese boxes all of wrought steel turning ceaselessly one within another'. This chapter can identify and open only some of the main boxes, but it begins a process that will continue with reading Woolf's works. Exploration of contexts becomes a matter of secondary as well as primary sources, and this chapter will offer guidance to the key publications for each context.

As an acclaimed high modernist writer, Woolf has not always been discussed in terms of context. Indeed, certain approaches to the context of modernism would encourage a purely formalist understanding of such writing. Yet what is so important about Woolf is that her immediate, intimate, intellectual context in Bloomsbury was itself the theoretical cradle of British formalism, and by extension, of formalist modernism. But Bloomsbury was also important as much for its practitioners as its theorists. Bloomsbury artists, such as Woolf's sister Vanessa Bell, for example, contributed much to Woolf's aesthetic development; and this contribution extended to her material context. She lived in the avant-garde domestic interiors her Bloomsbury colleagues created, and used furniture and fabrics designed and made by Bloomsbury's Omega Workshops.

If we consider Woolf's work in the context of feminist politics, on the other hand, we find that one of her most important contributions to feminist thought is itself directly concerned with context: *A Room of One's Own* (1929) puts the case for the development of private and public contexts conducive to the flourishing of women's writing. The coming of 'Shakespeare's sister', a great woman poet-playwright to rival Shakespeare, depends on women having access to private space in which to write, 'a room of one's own', but also access to public education and to professional life. *A Room of One's Own* considers the historical, political, social and literary contexts in which women's lives and women's writing are situated. *Three Guineas* (1938) examines these matters in the context of war, and mounts a feminist, pacifist argument against fascism.

In wider historical context, Woolf's life began in the Victorian age and ended in modern times, while her writing career spanned two world wars, cut short by her suicide at a particularly low point in the second. In her lifetime she experienced the social and political turbulence of the immense changes that occurred during the shift from the Victorian era to a self-consciously 'modern' era. Much of her writing is concerned with defining and describing modern life. But Woolf also enjoys an afterlife stretching from postwar culture to the present. Her image, her life story, her key sayings have been appropriated and recycled in all sorts of modern and contemporary contexts. Many of her works have been adapted for stage and screen. In attempting to understand in what contexts we are to understand Woolf, then, this chapter addresses firstly Woolf's biographies, which have in many ways been considerable influences on the contexts in which her writing is understood, and then considers how Woolf has been positioned in the context of Bloomsbury and its other members, in the wider historical and political contexts of her time, and in the context of modern and contemporary culture.

There are numerous biographies, images, mythologies, constructions, and accounts of Woolf as a person and a writer that have been generated in the past half-century or so. Most works on Woolf in her various contexts would fall into one of our four categories. Michael Whitworth's *Authors in Context: Virginia Woolf* (2005) offers more comprehensive, systematic contextual information in every category. His first three chapters explore Woolf's life, the social and political context of her life, and the literary scene in which she emerged. He then examines key novels by Woolf in the next three chapters in terms of philosophy, society, and science and medicine. His final chapter, 'Recontextualizing and Reconstructing Woolf', looks at recent film and stage adaptations and considers changing cultural interpretations of Woolf's life and work. Whitworth observes that 'reinterpretations of Woolf have themselves been complex and multi-stranded, bearing different meanings for different reading communities, and occasioning fierce debate between those who believe truly to understand her work' (226). A certain self-consciousness is demanded, then, of Woolf's readers, whether beginners or older hands. We must be aware of our own contexts and our own 'moments' (a key term for Woolf) for reading Woolf as much as we seek to understand the contexts and 'moments' she inhabited. Woolf herself writes with great sensitivity to the way one era may shape and filter another, and to the way the self shapes and is shaped by the moment:

> Yet what composed the present moment? If you are young, the future lies upon the present, like a piece of glass, making it tremble and quiver. If you are old, the past lies upon the present, like a thick glass, making it waver, distorting it. All the same, everybody believes that the present is something, seeks out different elements in this situation in order to compose the truth of it, the whole of it.   (*M* 9)

In attempting to capture Woolf, all commentators inevitably distort, making the glass quiver and waver. This chapter attempts to introduce the beginning reader to some of the recognised, larger ripples. Biographies of Woolf have made some of the largest ripples, providing some of the most influential frames of reference to her work and its reception.

Biographies

There are numerous biographies of Woolf. Biography has been highly influential in shaping the reception of Woolf's work, and her life has been as much debated as her writing. I would recommend the following three which represent three different biographical contexts and a range of positions on Woolf's life: Quentin Bell's *Virginia Woolf: A Biography* (1972), Hermione Lee's *Virginia Woolf* (1996), and Julia Briggs's *Virginia Woolf: An Inner Life* (2005). There is no one, true biography of Woolf (as, indeed, there cannot be of any subject of biography), but these three mark important phases in the writing and rewriting of Woolf's life. Hot debate continues over how biographers represent her mental health, her sexuality, her politics, her suicide, and of course her art, and over how we are to understand the latter in relation to all the former points of contention.

The first full-length and, for a long time, the most authoritative, biography is the two-volume work by her nephew Quentin Bell. Shortly before his death, Leonard Woolf invited Bell to write his wife's biography and gave him access to her private papers, including her diaries, five volumes of which Bell went on to edit and publish (1977–84). Leonard had allowed only a severely edited volume of selected entries from her diary to be published in 1953. Before the publication of her diaries and letters between 1975 and 1984, Bell's biography gave the ordinary reader unprecedented access to Woolf's private writings and the fullest account of her life. The first volume, *Virginia Stephen 1882–1912*, covers Woolf's childhood, family life and adulthood until her marriage in her thirtieth year. The second volume, *Mrs Woolf 1912–1941*, covers the second half of her life, during which time she remained happily married to Leonard and her writing career flourished. The chapters are organised chronologically, taking dates as their titles.

Although commissioned by Leonard Woolf, Bell's biography inevitably views its subject from the perspective and context of her sister's household rather than her own. Vanessa Bell's close bond with Woolf made her a source of great strength through Woolf's bouts of severe mental illness, and her son rightly emphasises her resilient and sustaining support during these very stressful periods:

> Virginia was an exceedingly difficult patient. Vanessa . . . had to scold, to exhort, to plead, in order that her sister might behave at *all* prudently. Sometimes bored to extinction and near to complete despair, sometimes recklessly euphoric about her health, Virginia was always adroit enough to use her charm upon her medical advisers so that she might win them over and make them her allies in whatever plot against routine and good sense she might devise. (*VWB1* 164)

Before marriage to Leonard, Vanessa was her sister's first point of refuge. After the death of their father in 1904, however, Woolf developed an irrational 'mistrust' of her sister. Bell's influential summary of Virginia's suicidal depression in that year declares: 'All that summer she was mad.' And having been nursed during this time by their friend Violet Dickinson, 'it was not until early September that she was able to leave . . ., thin and shaken, but sane enough to be able to live at peace with Vanessa' (*VWB1* 90). Bell's description of her symptoms at this time has been widely circulated: 'listening to the birds singing in Greek and imagining that King Edward VII lurked in the azaleas using the foulest possible language' (*VWB1* 90). His account of her death emphasises the onset of her 'madness' (*VWB2* 224).

Quentin Bell's biography is also a main source for the received opinion on Woolf's sexuality – or apparent lack of it. According to Bell she was 'frigid' (*VWB2* 6). He describes how her marriage to Leonard 'was not dependent upon the intenser joys of physical love' (*VWB2* 5). The sexual abuse she suffered from her half-brother is offered as partial explanation. Bell also invokes Woolf's lover Vita Sackville-West to confirm his view that Woolf 'regarded sex, not so much with horror, as with incomprehension; there was, both in her personality and in her art, a disconcertingly aetherial [*sic*] quality and, when necessities of literature compel her to consider lust, she either turns away or presents us with something as remote from the gropings and grapplings of the bed as is the flame of the candle from its tallow' (*VWB2* 6).

Such passages contributed to the popular myth of Virginia Woolf as a delicate, nun-like aesthete, incapable of sensual pleasure, and remote from the real world. Her letters and diaries belie this myth.

Bell also characterises Woolf as similarly unworldly in the sphere of politics, even in her antifascism during the 1930s:

> But were we then to scuttle like frightened spinsters before the fascist thugs? She belonged, inescapably, to the Victorian world of Empire, Class and privilege. Her gift was for the pursuit of shadows, for the ghostly whispers of the mind and for Pythian incomprehensibility, when what was needed was the swift and lucid phrase that could reach the ears of unemployed working men or Trades Union officials.   (*VWB2* 186)

Again, the myth of Woolf as ethereal, mystical and untouched by the real world is perpetuated. Leonard Woolf described his wife in his autobiography as 'the least political animal that has lived since Aristotle invented the description', [1] and Clive Bell remembered that 'Virginia was, in her peculiar way, an ardent feminist . . . in political feminism – the Suffrage Movement – she was not much interested.' [2] Bell later took the Woolf scholar Jane Marcus to task for her representation of Woolf as a Marxist feminist: 'Woolf wasn't a feminist and she wasn't political.' [3] Whatever we make of Bell's portrait of his aunt, his biography remains essential reading.

By the time Hermione Lee's *Virginia Woolf* (1996) appeared, two decades of feminist scholarship had already done much to unsettle and contest the received opinions emanating from Bell's biography. Lee's biography confirms Woolf as a feminist writer. Within the frame of four periods, Lee approaches the life through chapters devoted to topics rather than years. In 'Abuses' Lee attempts to correct the received view of Woolf as a 'victim' of childhood sexual abuse, a view initiated by Bell's biography and taken to psychobiographical extremes by Louise DeSalvo's sensationalist biography of 1989, *Virginia Woolf: The Impact of Childhood Sexual Abuse on Her Life and Work*, which reads Woolf's work as well as life through the lens of abuse. It is now, Lee acknowledges, 'impossible to think of this story [of Woolf's half-brothers' abuse] innocently, without being aware of what has been made of it'. Lee claims that

> what matters most in this story is what Virginia Woolf made out of what happened. Here the commentator can only point to the gap between the available evidence and the story she drew from it. There is no way of knowing whether the teenage Virginia Stephen was fucked or forced to have oral sex or buggered. Nor is it possible to say with certainty that these events . . . drove her mad.

And while 'Virginia Woolf herself thought that what had been done to her was very damaging', Lee suggests she 'would have been horrified by interpretations of her *work* which reduced it to a coded expression of neurotic symptoms' (*VWL* 158–9).

Lee also tilts against orthodox stereotypes of Woolf's 'insanity' in her chapter 'Madness', which opens with the assertion 'Virginia Woolf was a sane woman who had an illness.' She continues from the benchmark of Woolf's sanity:

> She was often a patient, but she was not a victim. She was not weak, or hysterical, or self-deluding, or guilty, or oppressed. On the contrary, she was a person of exceptional courage, intelligence and stoicism, who made the best use she could, and came to the deepest understanding possible to her, of her own condition. She endured, periodically, great agony of mind and severe physical pain, with remarkably little self-pity. (*VWL* 175)

Lee gives a more grounded picture of Woolf's early political interests and activities in 'Subversives', discussing her writing as 'always explicitly on the radical, subversive and modern side of [the] cultural divide', and finding her a subversive in her life in her involvement in the suffrage movement, the *Dreadnought* Hoax, and the Post-Impressionist exhibition (*VWL* 278–9). She also counters accusations of anti-Semitism made against Woolf and the 'derision of an ineffectual "Mrs Woolf", who wrote irrelevantly and uselessly about women's problems when something had to be done about Fascism'. On the contrary, Lee shows that, with regard to alleged anti-Semitism, Woolf 'spells out her complicity with bigotry and offensiveness by way of self-accusation and social critique' (*VWL* 680), pointing to Woolf's observation: '"How I hated marrying a Jew . . . what a snob I was"' (*L4* 194). With regard to her politics and antifascism, she shows Woolf's conception of a 'radical – and unpalatable – critique of "Hitler in England"', and her profile in the context of left-wing politics in the 1930s, and in the context of Leonard Woolf's political work for the left, pointing up how her political writings from this period have 'tended to be misunderstood and undervalued' (*VWL* 681).

Lee's treatment of Woolf's suicide has been admired for its detailed and sensitive account of its personal and political contexts. She shows that one myth that sprang up in the immediate aftermath of the suicide was that of the 'feeble, delicate lady authoress giving up on the war-effort' (*VWL* 766), as if Woolf had been somehow unpatriotic in giving up at this dark moment of the war. Leonard was obliged to write to the press explaining that 'she took her life, not because she could not "carry on", but because she thought she was going mad again and would not this time recover' (*VWL* 766). But over the decades a version of Woolf's suicide has circulated that makes no reference at all to the context of the war in which it occurred. The depiction of Woolf's suicide in the film *The Hours*, for example, is free of any such references. Lee discusses the 'careful, practical suicide plans' (*VWL* 730) that Leonard and Virginia had made for the event of a successful German invasion (both of them were on the Gestapo 'Black List'). Such information is often greeted with surprise by people who have absorbed received mythologies about Woolf's mental illness and suicide attempts. In her closing chapter, a self-conscious reflection on her own role and position as biographer, Lee concedes that 'disputes' that Woolf's life story arouses 'over madness, over modernism, over marriage' will of course continue, and that 'because of these re-appropriations, she seems to us, now, both a contemporary and a histor-ical figure' (*VWL* 769).

Nearly ten years on from Lee's biography, there are still new biographies of Woolf appearing, but Lee's has become the established benchmark for the generation of Woolf scholars who worked to uncover the Woolf that Quentin Bell's biography did not fully yield. Julia Briggs, in *Virginia Woolf: An Inner Life*, has achieved a timely return of focus to Woolf's life as a *writer*. Briggs's work is 'inspired by Woolf's own interest in the process of writing, as well as by a corresponding unease with accounts that . . . concentrate too narrowly on her social life, and so underestimate the centrality of her art – the main source of her interest for us' (*VWIL* x). Whereas Bell's chapters are organised according to dates, and Lee's by topic, Briggs refreshingly takes Woolf's published works as her organising principle. 'Woolf was evidently a highly sociable person,' she acknowledges, 'with a fascinating and gifted circle of family and friends, an engaging companion and an entrancing aunt, yet it was what she did when she was alone, walking or sitting at her desk, for which we now remember her' (*VWIL* x-xi). Briggs gives a fascinating portrait of Woolf as she creates her greatest works, showing and reflecting on the evolution of the creative process, and in each chapter offering a brief account of the 'aftermath', giving each book's publication and reception history.

Woolf's writing takes centre stage in this biography, but Briggs does discuss major life events, and squarely addresses Woolf's suicide, which she chooses to discuss in the context of other suicides by creative people during that period, such as Woolf's friend Mark Gertler, the painter, in 1939:

> Like other artists at that time, Gertler seems to have been overwhelmed by a combination of personal problems, a crisis in his own creativity and horror at the coming war. The old suffragist and pacificist Helena

> Swanwick . . . also committed suicide in 1939, apparently unable to bear
> the thought of another European war. The older sister of the painter
> Walter Sickert, she had been born in Bavaria.   (*VWIL* 398)

Briggs also cites a 'number of German writers, persecuted and exiled . . . who
took their own lives', including Ernst Toller whom Woolf knew, as well as
other European intellectuals such as Joseph Roth, Walter Benjamin, Stefan
Zweig and Simone Weil (*VWI* 398–9). Emphasis on such a context inflects
Woolf's suicide differently from either Bell or Lee, and again encourages us to
think of Woolf as a writer first and foremost, in the company of other great
writers, intellectuals and creative people of her age; a gesture that also lifts her
out of her immediate context in Bloomsbury.

Bloomsbury

Descriptions of the Bloomsbury Group, Woolf's famous circle of intellectual
and artistic colleagues, usually begin with Cambridge, and the elite group of
intellectuals, many of whom were in the society of Cambridge Apostles,
known to Woolf's elder brother Thoby. They were all greatly influenced by
the philosopher G. E. Moore, and also by Bertrand Russell. The Bloomsbury
Group included Lytton Strachey the critic and iconoclastic biographer of
Eminent Victorians (1918) and *Queen Victoria* (1921); the art critics Clive Bell
and Roger Fry, who introduced modern art to Britain in 1910 with their Post-
Impressionist exhibition and who developed highly influential formalist
theories of art; the influential radical economist John Maynard Keynes; and
Leonard Woolf, left-wing political theorist and publisher. Also in the circle
were the drama critic Desmond MacCarthy, the novelist E. M. Forster, the
painters Duncan Grant and Vanessa Bell, and Adrian Stephen, Woolf's
brother, an ardent pacifist who also dedicated himself to the advance of
psychoanalysis.

Details of major and peripheral Bloomsbury members are supplied by
Alan and Veronica Palmer's *Who's Who in Bloomsbury* (1987) and Mark
Hussey's *Virginia Woolf A to Z* (1995). Bloomsbury became synonymous
with avant-garde art, formalist aesthetics, libertine sexuality, radical thinking,
rational philosophy, progressive anti-imperialist and feminist politics, conscientious objection during the Great War, and antifascism in the 1930s. The
best introduction to the Bloomsbury Group is their own testimonies and
writings collected by S. P. Rosenbaum in *The Bloomsbury Group: A Collection
of Memoirs, Commentary, Criticism* (1975) and *A Bloomsbury Group Reader*

(1993). Rosenbaum is also responsible for the most detailed history of the group, in *Victorian Bloomsbury* (1987), *Edwardian Bloomsbury* (1994), and *Georgian Bloomsbury* (2003). Mary Ann Caws and Sarah Bird Wright have explored the group's links to the French art scene and excursions and residence in France in *Bloomsbury and France* (2000). Ann Banfield has explored the philosophical foundations and contexts of Bloomsbury in *The Phantom Table: Woolf, Fry, Russell and the Epistemology of Modernism* (2000).

Wider historical and political contexts

Woolf's life spanned Victorian and modern times. She was born in the year that Charles Darwin and Dante Gabriel Rossetti died (1882), and the broader historical and political contexts of her life include Queen Victoria's Diamond Jubilee (1897), the Boer War (1899–1902), suffragette riots, agitation for Irish Home Rule and widespread industrial action in Britain (1910–12), the Great War (1914–18), the Russian Bolshevik Revolution (1917), the execution of the Russian Tsar (1918), the establishment of the Irish Free State (1922), Mussolini's March on Rome (1922), the establishment of the Union of Soviet Socialist Republics (1923), the first Labour government in Britain (1924), the General Strike in Britain (1926), the collapse of the American stock exchange (1929), Hitler's appointment to the chancellorship of Germany and the burning of the Reichstag (1933), the British Abdication Crisis (1936), the Spanish Civil War (1936) and the destruction of Guernica (1937), the start of the Second World War (1939), and the London Blitz (1940). She did not live to witness the apocalypse of the Nazi gas chambers nor the dropping of atomic bombs on Hiroshima and Nagasaki (1945).

The cultural and intellectual contexts of Woolf's life include the development and accessibility of transport, and huge increases in its speed; the emergence of visible and invisible communications such as photography, the cinema, the telephone, telegraphy and the wireless, which resulted in the rapid transmission of news, ideas and images on a scale previously unknown; the discoveries of X-rays and radium; the artificial generation of electricity and its use in everyday life; and not least discoveries and hypotheses about the structure of matter, space and time, and about the processes of perception, and the understanding of the self.

Whitworth's *Authors in Context: Virginia Woolf* attempts to make sense of Woolf's life and writing in terms of many of these historical, political and cultural contexts. Alex Zwerdling's influential book *Virginia Woolf and the*

Real World (1986) was one of the first to situate Woolf and her writing in such contexts, and the historical turn in literary criticism since the 1990s has encouraged a flood of books examining Woolf and her writing in historical context. Mark Hussey's collection, *Virginia Woolf and War: Fiction, Reality and Myth* (1991), for example, focuses on Woolf in the context of the Great War, the Spanish Civil War, and the Second World War. Karen L. Levenback confines her gaze to the first of these in *Virginia Woolf and the Great War* (1999). Melba Cuddy-Keane, in *Virginia Woolf, the Intellectual, and the Public Sphere* (2003), examines Woolf's historical place as a publicly engaged intellectual who contributed as a writer and teacher to democratic movements in education and culture. Cuddy-Keane shows in detail how Woolf enriched the public debates of her time, revealing her as a writer firmly embedded in the public sphere, rather than removed from it, as myths of her modernist elitism would have it. In Pamela Caughie's collection of essays, *Virginia Woolf in the Age of Mechanical Reproduction* (2000), a number of leading Woolf scholars examine Woolf's work in the context of the emergent new technologies (cinema, photography, radio, the gramophone, and so on) and of the mass culture and mass communication of her own time as well as looking at Woolf in the context of contemporary technologies and communication.

Modern and contemporary cultural contexts

It has taken six decades since her death for Virginia Woolf to become Hollywood box-office gold. Nicole Kidman's portrayal, in Stephen Daldry's film *The Hours* (2002), of the author in the period when she was writing her famous novel *Mrs Dalloway* (1922), as well as, more sensationally, of her suicidal exit by drowning in 1941, is commercial, mainstream cinematic confirmation of Woolf's powerful and turbulent cultural afterlife. *The Hours*, based on the novel of the same name by Michael Cunningham, not only plays fast and loose with Woolf's life, suggesting links between her mental illness, her creativity and an implied repressed lesbianism, it also attempts to show the impact of Woolf's writing on a woman reader in patriarchal, postwar America, and explores the progress of gender and sexual politics since the time of *Mrs Dalloway*, transposing it to the gay and lesbian scene in contemporary New York. However erroneous its portrayal of Woolf herself, the film nevertheless demonstrates her enduring and powerful influence on modern mores.

Brenda Silver, in *Virginia Woolf Icon* (1999), remarks on how 'in the popular realm, continual enactments and reenactments of Virginia Woolf as name, image, spectacle, fashion, or performance have become the norm'.[4]

She traces the 'multiple, contradictory sites [Woolf] occupies in our cultural discourses: British intellectual aristocrat, high modernist, canonical author, writer of best-sellers, Bloomsbury liberal, Labour Party socialist, feminist, sapphist, acknowledged beauty, suicide, and woman'.[5] She comments on the cultural phenomenon whereby people who have never knowingly read a word by Virginia Woolf can confidently relate (while fatuously citing the title of Edward Albee's famous play, *Who's Afraid of Virginia Woolf?*) that she was mad, a snob, and committed suicide. It here seems necessary (even now) to modify these observations by noting that although Woolf endured a number of episodes of insanity, she seems to have enjoyed a full and productive creative and social life with long periods free of illness; that she was capable of sending up her own snobbery ('I am not only a coronet snob; but also a lit up drawing room snob; a social festivity snob' (*MOB* 210)); and that her suicide was not as youthful as Sylvia Plath's, occurring when she was nearly sixty and no longer much resembling the young beauty of the famous G. C. Beresford photograph in the National Portrait Gallery, and at a harrowing time of national emergency (the German bombardment of Britain during the Second World War), a context entirely missing from Daldry's film. Silver puts the case for Woolf's double cultural afterlife, showing how her image has been put to work in straddling high and low culture, however much a certain sector of academe seeks to preserve the myth of Woolf as a remote, elitist aesthete.

Woolf has also been on the receiving end of considerable academic scorn. In her lifetime she was attacked with vitriol in the pages of *Scrutiny* by F. R. Leavis and Q. D. Leavis, and their legacy lingers with academics such as Tom Paulin, who mounted a similarly hysterical assault in his television programme *J'Accuse* (1991), when she was vilified as a snob and a bigot in her private life and without talent in her writing. But such assaults again serve to indicate the potency of Woolf's iconic status in contemporary culture. Whereas Silver's book offers a serious account of Woolf's shifting and contradictory iconic status, and uses this to probe wider political issues in contemporary Anglo-American culture, Regina Marler's book, *Bloomsbury Pie* (1997), has given some playful insight into Woolf and the rise of the 'Bloomsbury industry', and into the wars between different factions in Woolf studies. Both books show that there are multiple versions of Virginia Woolf available, reflecting myriad shades of critical, theoretical and political positions.

It is worth emphasising, however, that although Woolf's work and life have been mediated, since her death, by hordes of specialist and academic critical and cultural aficionados, it should be remembered that in her lifetime she was a successful, bestselling author, whose reading public bought and read her work without the benefits, or otherwise, of such mediation. Not only was her 'light' novel, *Flush: A Biography*, enormously popular (to the later embarrassment of some high-minded critics), but her 'high modernist' novels also did very well in the marketplace. From the proceeds of the first edition of *To the Lighthouse*, for example, Woolf was able to buy a new car. And as the title of her two *Common Reader* collections of essays, suggests, her nonfiction also sold well, and to a wide audience. Her feminist polemic, *A Room of One's Own*, itself the foundation for modern feminist literary, cultural and political theories, in all their sometimes arcane complexities, still often surprises readers with its entertaining, readable and playful style. That this text is now deemed inaccessible without specialist professional help seems ironic considering that it addresses the fact, at the time of writing, of most women's exclusion from university education and from the professions, and from mainstream as well as highbrow literary discourse. As Chapter Three will show, much of Woolf's own critical writing is framed to help readers understand and appreciate the nuances and 'difficulties' of new, avant-garde literary practices.

Twenty-first-century readers of Woolf, however, do need some guidance through the various contexts in which Woolf's fiction and nonfiction may be placed, precisely because of the enormous impact Woolf's oeuvre has had, and precisely because of the conflicting myths, narratives and images of Woolf that have permeated modern culture as a result of this impact. Beginning readers of Woolf need orientation through the enormous array of related critical, cultural and biographical material available to those who wish to go beyond the primary texts. This chapter on contexts has suggested starting places for reading Woolf in the context of biography, in the context of Bloomsbury, and in wider historical and contemporary contexts. *The Hours* marks a sea-change, in some respects, in pervasive Woolfian stereotypes, and in received wisdom on Woolf. More than a decade after Paulin's damaging television programme, Woolf has again risen to become an icon of cultural and intellectual celebrity chic. It is a mark of her enormous importance, her continuing, and refreshing, relevance as an artist that she has been treated to such extremes in the media. Audiences of *Basic Instinct 2* (2006), for example, are clearly deemed *au fait* enough with Woolf's and Bloomsbury's charged reputations to grasp the film's hilarious cultural referencing. The protagonist, a psychopathic and sexually predatory female novelist, played by Sharon Stone, who takes the nom de plume Woolf, having survived suicidal drowning, torments her Bloomsbury psychiatrist to the point of his own insanity. Yet again, Woolf is invoked to unsettle high and popular culture.

Works

Virginia Woolf's oeuvre is sizable. Most of her writings, across several genres, are in print, including a growing number of holograph, draft and facsimile editions of key works. While the latter are probably not of immediate interest to those starting to read Woolf, it is the case that her letters, diaries, memoirs and essays may well be studied along with her novels and short stories. But it is Woolf's achievement as a novelist that firstly marks her out as a major modern writer. This chapter will focus mainly on the ten novels in chronological order from *The Voyage Out* (1915) to *Between the Acts* (1941), and a selection of stories, then turn to Woolf's key works of literary criticism, concentrating mainly on *A Room of One's Own* (1929) and a selection of essays. Woolf's autobiographical writings are drawn on throughout this book, particularly where they are relevant to Woolf's biography or to those works prioritised for introductory discussion. But they might nevertheless be understood as important works in themselves, not only as resources for illustrating the life or compositional processes. The first section of this chapter focuses on Woolf's fiction, the second section on her nonfiction.

Woolf's writing demands close scrutiny by its readers. Before turning to the works themselves, let us briefly note how we might approach them, and what some of the basic, common approaches to studying Woolf have been. Some works are considered difficult and challenging because of their obvious experimentalism with form, but even in these, as well as in the less experimental works, Woolf's writing may also appear disarmingly simple; and such writing is no less demanding of careful attention. In the context of writing about modernist literature in general elsewhere, I have recommended two critical and theoretical questions that we should ask of the texts of this period: (1) 'Who is speaking?'; and (2) 'Where is she?' 'Who is speaking?' is a question derived from one of the most important and influential critics writing on the literature of this period, Erich Auerbach, and the question he asks of a particular paragraph in Woolf's novel *To the Lighthouse* (1927). This is an excellent question to ask of modernist and avant-garde texts, not only to establish perspectives on their often complex narrative points of view, and so on. It is an essential question to ask of experimental and multivocal texts that so frequently juxtapose citations and quotations from other sources, and so often give voice to other writers, living and dead, as well as to discourses and ideologies from such diverse other quarters – social, political, scientific, psychoanalytical, artistic and musical. Is modernity speaking, or is tradition speaking, we might also ask. 'Who is speaking?' is also an essential question to ask of experimental texts that seek to explore and produce new models of the self, identity and subjectivity.

'Where is she?' is a question taken from the influential theorist of gender Hélène Cixous. Not only does it supplement the question 'Who is speaking?' with the thought 'Is *he* or *she* speaking?', it also points up the questions of how language itself may be gendered, and how *literary* language may be gendered. If the literature of the period, whether by women or men, is concerned with inventing and developing new, conflicting and transformational modernist and avant-garde languages, it may well be concerned with how such languages are gendered, and with what kinds of gendered subjectivity they record and produce.

These questions are helpful ones to ask when we read Woolf's writing, whether fiction, literary criticism, biography, autobiography or polemic.

Woolf's fiction

In the following introductory discussion of the novels, certain key terms and issues recur as touchstones. Each novel is inflected differently, but they have many interconnections. As well as understanding them broadly in terms of modernism and feminism, and in terms of Woolf's oppositional language encapsulated in her phrase 'granite and rainbow' (fact and fiction, prose and poetry, art and life), we may also approach Woolf's novels with an eye on her experiment with genre. Some of her novels may be understood as experiments in the Bildungsroman (a novel charting an individual's development) or in the Künstlerroman (a novel charting an artist's development) or in biography, individual and collective; some sport the formal features of satire and elegy, some come closer to poetry than fiction.

Each novel is introduced below broadly in terms of subject matter and style, and with reference to the relevant places in Woolf's diaries and letters where she comments on their composition. Discussion of each novel will also touch on key points for critical interpretation, and indicate a sense of the immediate and early reception of each novel. Four sample pieces of criticism offer different ways to approach further reading. Following the critical questions suggested above, and as a general guide to approaching Woolf's fiction, I would recommend thinking about each work in terms of the broad concerns in literary criticism that Woolf's writing has helped to frame and that shape many approaches to her fiction: for example, modernist concerns with form and aesthetics, feminist concerns with gender, sexuality, subjectivity, and how such concerns relate to matters of form and representation.

To begin with, readers of Woolf's fiction might consult Woolf's own influential criticism, key samples of which are discussed later in this section. 'Modern Fiction' and 'Mr Bennett and Mrs Brown', for example, are standard texts in modernist approaches, and *A Room of One's Own* a major source for feminist and gender approaches. Many other approaches and critical debates follow from these mainsprings in Woolf criticism: readings concerned with class, race, the literary canon, literary allusions, the influence of the visual arts, and so on. Each novel is discussed below with reference to these broad issues.

The setting of each novel is also worth careful consideration. These are imaginary, literary places, even the London that appears in several of her works. Woolf singled out in her notebook William Blake's comment on Wordsworth: 'Natural objects always did and now do weaken, deaden, & obliterate imagination in me'; and in a review of Edward Thomas's *A Literary Pilgrim in England* (1917), she finds 'the poets and the counties are connected on the most elastic and human principle; and if in the end it turns out that the poet was not born there, did not live there, or quite probably had no place at all in his mind when he wrote, his neglect is shown to be quite as characteristic as his sensibility' (*E2* 161). Woolf chose to set *To the Lighthouse* in Scotland, which she did not visit until many years after it was written. There are obvious autobiographical references to her childhood holidays in Cornwall in that novel, but it would obliterate its imaginative power to insist that the Hebrides should be ignored and read merely as a thin cipher for Cornwall. *The Voyage Out* is set in South America, a place Woolf never visited. Like Woolf herself, Blake 'comes under London and the Home Counties' and, she reminds us

> it is true that, as it is necessary to live somewhere, he lived both in London and at Felpham, near Bognor. But there is no reason to think that the tree that was filled with angels was peculiar to Peckham Rye, or that the bulls that "each morning drag the sulphur Sun out of the Deep" [Blake, *Milton* I.21.20] were to be seen in the fields of Sussex.   (*E2* 161–2)[1]

There is no reason to think that the lighthouse in *To the Lighthouse* entirely corresponds to the Godrevy lighthouse that Woolf saw as a child. It is also the case that both Blake and Woolf did also write specifically and compellingly about London. But it would be naïve and diminishing to ignore the imaginative and symbolic dimensions with which both writers infuse their London locations. Quoting Blake's note on the deadening effect of natural objects, Woolf approves Thomas's openness to a statement 'which might have annoyed a specialist determined to pin a poet down'. If this 'is a fine opening into the mind of Blake' (*E2* 162), it may well serve as a fine opening to Woolf's, too. Knowledge of Woolf's personal biography, of the locations she lived in and visited certainly enriches our reading, but her writing should not be entirely pinned down by it either.

The Voyage Out (1915)

Woolf's first novel contains many of the self-conscious, stylised features of a Bildungsroman, or a Künstlerroman (since it charts the life, development and education of a musician). Woolf later thought it 'a harlequinade' and 'assortment of patches' (*D2* 17). Writing it, she wanted to 're-form the novel' and 'capture multitudes of things at present fugitive' (*L1* 356). She sets out, then, to challenge conventional fictional form and to stretch the inclusive capacity of conventional fictional content. Both style and subject matter are to be new departures for the novel. Yet the modern patchwork method she found, while subtly pronounced, is not radical nor entirely new. Patchwork is in fact a standard feature of traditional satire, which is classically defined as *satura lanx* (a mixed dish). And the novel often patches quite traditional and familiar fictional matter. The reader of *The Voyage Out* may gain a false sense of narratological security from such familiar points of reference, but then be turned in the next sentence or paragraph on to more treacherous ground, if only because a different set of familiar fictional codes appear to be adopted. The very title, so optimistic in one sense, particularly for a debut novel, is also sinisterly suggestive of a journey that will take us away from the familiar and leave us stranded, unable to return, the fate in fact of its unhappy protagonist. The matter of its setting is also contentious. The ostensible destination of the sea-voyage in *The Voyage Out* is a fictional British colony in South America. Her handling of the representation of this location (not one she knew from personal experience), suggests that Woolf is patching diverse textual sources rather than attempting accurate realisation of South American geography or people.

The Voyage Out, set in 1905, concerns the journey that Rachel Vinrace, a musically talented but socially isolated, and motherless, young woman, makes to South America on her father Willoughby Vinrace's vessel the *Euphrosyne* (which not only refers to the Greek goddess, the Grace of Joy, but is also Woolf's dig at the privately published collection of rather bad poetry by Clive Bell, Leonard Woolf, Lytton Strachey and others that appeared under this title in 1905). Its opening scene on the embankment of the Thames echoes that of Joseph Conrad's *Heart of Darkness* (1902), a key reference in Woolf's narrative frame. The Conservative politician Dalloway and his wife Clarissa (who reappear in Woolf's fourth novel, *Mrs Dalloway*) join the boat for a while before disembarking on the African coast. The naïve Rachel, treated to his reactionary views on women's suffrage and art, is greatly disturbed by Dalloway's sexual advances towards her during a storm. Recommending to her the counter-revolutionary writings of Edmund Burke, he 'kissed her passionately, so that she felt the hardness of his body' (*VO* 66). This distressing encounter, combining unwanted sexual attention with a lesson in reactionary, imperialist politics, induces in Rachel a nightmare in which she is trapped in a vault with a 'deformed' and 'gibbering' man (*VO* 68).

The vault imagery and other references allude to the classical legend of Antigone (a figure of some interest to feminist thinkers), the daughter of Oedipus who, in Sophocles' play, commits suicide having been entombed alive by the tyrant Creon for defying his diktat not to bury her brother. Dalloway's kiss also prefigures the somewhat sinister, vampiric kiss, in the novel's penultimate deathbed scene, of Rachel's fiancé, Terence, whose name may be linked to that of another mythic tyrant, Tereus. Woolf frequently alludes in her writings to the myth of Tereus, who raped Philomela, the sister of his wife Procne, and then cut out her tongue. Rachel's death in Terence's embrace is also attended by hallucinations alluding to Antigone's fate.

Under the wing of her aunt, Helen, wife of classical scholar Ridley Ambrose, Rachel's social horizons are broadened by her stay in South America. The action in the fictional Santa Marina occurs mainly among the English colonials there, in the Ambroses' villa and the hotel, a setting conducive to traditional country house-style fiction. (This is where Joseph Conrad meets Jane Austen in Woolf's prose.) In Santa Marina, Rachel meets, among others, Mr Wilfred Flushing, a dealer in primitive art, and his wife Alice, an artist of exuberant temperament, and two somewhat patronising young Cambridge Englishmen of intimidating intellect, St John Hirst and Terence Hewet. Once established, Rachel goes on a second journey, instigated by the Flushings, upriver to visit a native village. Rachel falls in love with and becomes engaged to Hewet, an aspiring writer, whose ambition it is to 'write a novel about Silence' (*VO* 204). Silence is a key issue in Woolf's own writing. Rachel finds herself tutored by Hirst, another tyro writer, in reading Edward Gibbon's *The History of the Decline and Fall of the Roman Empire* (1776–88). Hirst himself is found reading Swinburne's translation of the classical poet Sappho in church, and later drafts sacrilegious poetry.

In a novel peppered with allusions to canonical literature (including Sophocles, Hakluyt, Shakespeare, Wordsworth, Austen, Scott and Conrad), Rachel falls into a silent and fatal swoon while listening, in the heat of the sun, to her fiancé read Milton's masque poem *Comus* (such is the power of poetry!). After some time in a state of hallucinatory fever and then coma, she dies in his embrace. The 'Lady' of Milton's allegory evades rape and breaks Comus's subsequent spell with the aid of saving wave sent by the river-goddess Sabrina (*VO* 309). There is no medical explanation for Rachel's mysterious and fatal illness. The allusions to *Antigone* bring the whiff of suicide, but this is never overtly suggested. Whereas the mind of Keats, 'that very fiery particle', according to Byron, 'let itself be snuffed out by an Article' (*Don Juan* XI.60)[2], Rachel seems to have been killed off by *Comus*. At any rate, her reading, as much as her social and sexual induction, seems to be to blame.

'What I wanted to do', Woolf reflects, 'was to give the feeling of a vast tumult of life, as various and disorderly as possible, which should be cut short for a moment by the death, and so go on again – and the whole was to have a sort of pattern' (*L2* 82). Rachel's sorry fate, then, has a formal function for Woolf, and it becomes a measure of that of the surviving minor characters, such as the submissive and conformist Susan Warrington who happily becomes engaged to Arthur Venning, another social conformist; and is contrasted by the enthusiasm and optimism of the nonconforming left-wing suffragist and aspiring revolutionary Evelyn Murgatroyd, who dodges several marriage proposals and is intent on travelling to revolutionary Moscow at the close of the novel. But Rachel's death suggests that there is no social or political space for a young woman such as her to flourish as an artist while also entering a marriage, particularly one with the conventionally accultur-ated Hewet. The stylised story of Rachel's personal development, romantic courtship and then decline, however, is simultaneously a structural device that allows the novel to expose and critique the workings of the British imperialist and class system in which she is caught up.

Woolf's impressive first novel was a long time in its conception and creation. She drafted and redrafted this 'work of the Fancy and the Affections' (*L1* 331), as she called it in 1908, under the provisional title of 'Melymbrosia', and came to a methodology based, not on 'rhapsodis[ing]', but on the recognition that the best novels are 'deposited, carefully, bit by bit' (*L1* 350). Clive Bell, responding to a draft in 1909, thought it very promising but objected to a perceived didacticism concerning her portrayal of men and women. Woolf defended her 'prejudice against men' on the grounds that 'a man, in the present state of the world, is not a very good judge of his sex', and she confirms her work as 'represent[ing] roughly a view of one's own' (*L1* 383). By 1910 Woolf writes of how she is 'seething with fragments of love, morals, ethics, comedy tragedy' (*L1* 440) which gives a sense of the novel's poignant analysis of the gender politics of courtship and marriage.

Her announcement of her engagement to Leonard Woolf (whom she married in 1912) coincided with her finishing the novel, and between his submission of the manuscript to Gerald Duckworth in March 1913 and its publication two years later, Woolf suffered suicidal bouts of depression and severe misgivings about her work and its reception: 'everyone will assure me [it] is the most brilliant thing they've ever read; & privately condemn, as indeed it deserves to be condemned' (*D1* 29). She feared she would be considered a 'failure as a writer, as well as a failure as a woman' (*L1* 499). Like many first novels, it represents the writer's sense of coming out as an artist. As her exchanges with Clive Bell indicate, it is the sexual and gender politics attending the debut of the emergent modern woman novelist that inform its very conception. Woolf identifies herself as 'a painstaking woman who wishes to treat of life as she finds it, and to give voice to some of the perplexities of her sex' (*L1* 381), a somewhat reserved restatement of her novel's feminist agenda. The novel may also have been influenced by concerns about Empire and colonialism, as raised by Leonard Woolf's novel written in the same period, *The Village in the Jungle* (1913).

Like James Joyce's *A Portrait of the Artist as a Young Man* (1916), Woolf's first novel is a self-conscious meditation on the formation of an emergent intellectual and artist (a Künstlerroman). One of the guests at the hotel is Miss Allan, a teacher of English who is writing 'a short *Primer of English Literature* – Beöwulf to Swinburne' (*VO* 93). Miss Allan is absorbed by Wordsworth's *Prelude* (*VO* 93), the subtitle of which is 'The Growth of a Poet's Mind'. As in Joyce's novel, the reading and education of Woolf's protagonist is a central occupation. But unlike Stephen Dedalus, the protagonist of *The Voyage Out* dies before reaching maturity and with no prospect, even had she survived and therefore married, of fulfilling her ambitions as a musician. These fatal gender politics seem augured by the disruption to Miss Allan's attention on the very apt Book Five of the *Prelude* (its title 'Books' is not directly given), caused by the sound of material gender conformity: 'a swishing sound next door – a woman, clearly, putting away her dress' and 'a gentle tapping sound, such as that which accompanies hair-dressing' (*VO* 93). Rachel's engagement to Terence is presented as crushing her artistic potential and development so that he may flourish. So saturated is this narrative with literary, aesthetic, mythical and cultural allusions that it demands to be read in terms of its subtle, self-consciousness experimentalism. *The Voyage Out* does not attempt a realist account of its sea-voyage or of its South American setting, making obvious play with selections from the Elizabethan Richard Hakluyt's classic *Collection of the Early Voyages, Travels, and Discoveries of the English Nation* (which Woolf read in 1897) and with Conrad's *Heart of Darkness*, and offering stylised pastoral vignettes of a painterly landscape that owes something to the Post-Impressionist art of Paul Gauguin promoted by Woolf's Bloomsbury colleagues.

Rachel's aunt and mentor, Helen Ambrose, is depicted consulting the work of G. E. Moore, whose philosophy influenced Bloomsbury, while she works an embroidery of 'a great design of a tropical river running through a tropical forest, where spotted deer would eventually browse upon masses of fruit, bananas, oranges, and giant pomegranates, while a troop of naked natives whirled darts into the air'. This needlework, a proleptic indication of Rachel's later journey to the interior 'native village', speaks of both Elizabethan representations of foreign ventures and Gauguin's sensual orientalist art. Woolf's narrative self-consciously interweaves references to Bloomsbury intellectualism by relating how 'between the stitches' of this work Mrs Ambrose 'looked to one side and read a sentence about the Reality of Matter, or the Nature of Good' (*VO* 25). This juxtaposition of diverse cultural references reflects Woolf's own methodology and her conception of the novel as 'an assortment of patches' (*D2* 17). The stitching Mrs Ambrose also personifies a conventional view of women's creativity, and she is described in the context of a busy decklife in which men occupy themselves, working in all sorts of capacities, or merely idle, a sampling of empire's labourers, administrators, scholars and traders: 'men in blue jerseys' who 'scrubbed the boards, or leant over the rails and whistled', the Cambridge bachelor scholar, Mr Pepper (ex-India), who 'sat cutting up roots with a penknife', Ridley Ambrose, the classical scholar, 'at his Greek', and Willoughby Vinrace himself, ex-Cambridge, head of a shipping line and aspiring politician, who is 'at his documents' of business (*VO* 25).

A later scene, in the native village, also observes gender-divided labour. In this equally stylised vignette, there are no 'naked natives whirl[ing] darts' (*VO* 25), but there is a stereotyped 'primitive' (*VO* 81) scene, in which the politics of looking is explored. Arriving 'through the trees' in sight of 'strange wooden nests', Rachel and Terence are 'observ[ing] the women, who were squatting on the ground in triangular shapes, moving their hands, either plaiting straw or in kneading something in bowls' (*VO* 269). The reduction of the women to 'triangular shapes' suggests the aesthetics of Post-Impressionist painting where composition is structured through primary geometric forms. (Compare the modern painter Lily Briscoe's portrait of a mother and child as a purple triangle in *To the Lighthouse.*) But the women stare back 'with the motionless inexpressive gaze of those removed from each other far far beyond the plunge of speech' (*VO* 269), suggesting that the white tourists are ineffably strange objects themselves. The intruders are described 'peer[ing]', as if at exhibits in an imperial showcase, 'into the huts where they could distinguish guns leaning in the corner, and bowls upon the floor, and stacks of rushes', but the returning stare, 'curiously not without hostility', of the people exhibited seems to unnerve and shame them: 'As she drew apart her shawl and uncovered her breast to the lips of her baby, the eyes of a woman never left their faces, although they moved uneasily under her stare, and finally turned away, rather than stand there looking at her any longer' (*VO* 269). The sight of the apparently contemptuous returning gaze of a mother intimately occupied in feeding her child drives them away. It is a visual riposte to the misogynist Hirst's earlier declared abhorrence of 'the female breast. Imagine being Venning and having to get into bed with Susan!' (*VO* 190). Indigenous South American people are represented by a patch- work of Western aesthetic references to the 'primitive' (*VO* 76, 81, 224) and construed as a vehicle, or a mirror, for Rachel and Terence to reflect on their own relationship: 'Seeking each other, Terence and Rachel drew together' (*VO* 265).

Immediately before this village scene, Rachel is described in delirious embrace with Helen Ambrose, who 'was upon her', and Rachel is 'rolled this way and that' before they are joined by Terence (*VO* 268). Anticipating Clarissa Dalloway's nostalgia, in the later novel *Mrs Dalloway*, for a lost moment of lesbian encounter, this fleeting, erotically charged moment be- tween the women suggests an alternative sexuality that Rachel is barred from exploring, and renders highly ironic Helen's intervention as the marital agent between Rachel and Terence. If this hazy moment represents a brief glimpse of a lost alternative, the nightmares that accompany Rachel after her engage- ment to Terence dominate the novel. The nightmares, however, do not emanate from the primitivist tableau representing the South American interior, but from the heart of patriarchal imperialism, triggered by the imperialist kiss of Richard Dalloway, and brought on further by her fiancé's reading of *Comus*. Ominously, the novel closes with the dreamlike and reifying vision of the misogynist Hirst, 'across [whose] eyes passed a procession of objects, black and indistinct, the figures of people picking up their books, their cards, their balls of wool, their work-baskets, and passing him one after another on their way to bed' (*VO* 347).

The Voyage Out was greeted by Lytton Strachey as 'very, very unvictorian!' and its handling 'divine', but he felt it 'lacked the cohesion of a dominating idea'[3]. This sense of a promising but flawed debut characterises much of the novel's early reception. Whereas the *New Statesman* reviewer thought that it had 'incisive description . . . satire and wit' while lacking 'humanity which ought to pull the whole together' (*CH* 56), E. M. Forster's review found that *The Voyage Out* does 'attain unity', and invoking *Wuthering Heights* for comparison, describes it as 'recklessly feminine'. Forster identifies 'one serious defect' in that her 'chief characters are not vivid' (*CH* 52–3). Woolf went on to address the function of 'character' in fiction in a number of essays, notably ('Modern Fiction' and 'Mr Bennett and Mrs Brown'), which would suggest that Forster's looking for conventional character and characterisation in her work is beside the point. Forster judged successful the novel's allegory of human 'adventure': 'It is for a voyage into solitude that man was created, and Rachel, Helen, Hewet, Hirst, all learn this lesson, which is exquisitely reinforced by the setting of tropical scenery – the soul, like the body, voyages at her own risk' (*CH* 54).

As critics have been debating ever since, *The Voyage Out* may be understood as many kinds of allegory: an allegory of skewed sexual and emotional discovery, an allegory of thwarted artistic endeavour, an allegory of women's thwarted progress in patriarchy. But these may be limiting readings. The novel so clearly self-consciously disrupts unified allegorical interpretations. We must also consider how far the voyage to a fictional South American colony is a metaphor that serves merely to explore individual emotional and psychological development; and how far the narrative of emotional and psychological development is itself functioning metaphorically as a means to explore and satirise ideologies and discourses of imperialism and colonialism. Whereas Forster is concerned by Woolf's apparently inadequate representation of her 'chief characters', recent critics are concerned by her racially stereotyped representation of the indigenous South American people who inhabit the 'setting of tropical scenery' that Forster finds so 'exquisitely reinforc[ing]' of the humanist, spiritual voyage undertaken by the four main white characters.

The many extant drafts of *The Voyage Out* have been explored by critics, and have informed some readings of the published novel. There is a wealth of material on the nature and meaning of Woolf's process of revision. An edition of the draft, *Melymbrosia*, has been published, which presents one editor's version of Woolf's avant-texte. The status of the text of *The Voyage*

Out itself is further complicated by Woolf's quite substantial revisions for the American edition of 1920.

Suggested further reading

Louise DeSalvo, *Virginia Woolf's First Voyage: A Novel in the Making* (Totowa, NJ: Rowman & Littlefield, 1980)

Madeline Moore, 'Some Female Versions of Pastoral: *The Voyage Out* and Matriarchal Mythologies', in Jane Marcus (ed.), *New Feminist Essays on Virginia Woolf* (Lincoln and London: University of Nebraska Press, 1981), pp. 82–104

Kathy Phillips, *Virginia Woolf Against Empire* (Knoxville: University of Tennessee Press, 1994)

Carey Snider, 'Woolf's Ethnographic Modernism: Self-Nativizing in *The Voyage Out* and Beyond' *Woolf Studies Annual* 10 (2004), pp. 81–108

Night and Day (1919)

Woolf's second novel is conventional in form, and her longest piece of fiction. It is dedicated to her sister, Vanessa Bell, on whom the heroine, Katharine Hilbery, is partly modelled. Woolf regarded this romantic comedy as another apprentice piece, a means of learning 'what to leave out: by putting it all in' (*L6* 216). This 'novel of fact' (*D4* 129), as she later termed it, seems to mimic nineteenth-century realism even as it outlines the passing of all things Victorian. Yet it also has its fair share of literary allusions that suggest a modernist self-consciousness at work. Katharine Hilbery is the daughter – like Woolf – of an upper-middle-class intellectual household in London. She is assisting her mother in writing the biography of her grandfather, a famous poet. Mrs Hilbery is also chasing a fantasy that Ann Hathaway was the author of Shakespeare's sonnets. At one point the setting switches to a country house, reminiscent of a Jane Austen novel. There is a schematic oppositional symbolism at work in *Night and Day*, as its title suggests; and it underpins Woolf's playful engagement with her traditional courtship plot. The novel's draft title was 'Dreams and Realities', which indicates a satirical approach to the gap between the dominant ideology of courtship and the real lived experience of it. It soon becomes evident that traditional gender roles, for men and women, are being explored and subtly undermined.

Katharine herself reverses gender stereotypes in her closet activity as mathematician-astronomer, enjoying a secret 'unwomanly' nocturnal life of rationalism. She is courted by William Rodney, an aspiring poet and becomes engaged to him, while simultaneously becoming involved in an emotional triangle with Ralph Denham, a lawyer who writes for the *Critical Review*, and Mary Datchet, a suffragist experiencing difficulties with the feminist 'cause', who is attracted to Katharine and in love with Ralph (and responsible for educating him in radical politics). At one point Mary refuses Ralph's proposal of marriage; and after the usual such obstacles, mistaken pairings and misunderstandings, Katharine and Ralph become engaged at the close of the novel. William falls for Katharine's cousin Cassandra, and they become engaged after Katharine and William admit to their mismatch. Mary, the suffragist turned socialist, remains single, and in the final chapter Katharine and Ralph gaze up at her window, but decide not to disturb her.

Woolf wrote a good deal of *Night and Day* while convalescing from depression in bed and restricted to writing 'for only one half hour a day' (*L4* 231); and looking back in the 1930s on this anomalous and 'interminable' novel, she thought that it 'taught me certain elements of composition which I should not have had the patience to learn had I been in the full flush of health always' (*L4* 231). On its completion in 1919, however, she thought it 'a much more mature & finished book than The Voyage Out' (*D1* 259). She conceived it, she claims, from an interest in the question 'of the things one doesn't say; what effect does that have? And how far do our feelings take their colour from the dive underground?' (*L2* 400) In this way, *Night and Day* resembles Terence Hewet's projected 'novel about Silence' (*VO* 204) in *The Voyage Out*; and there is a sense of unspoken or hidden, cryptic meanings in *Night and Day*.

Katharine, for example, regards her secret nocturnal life of 'unwomanly' scientific inquiry as 'directly opposed to literature. She would not have cared to confess how infinitely she preferred the exactitude, the star-like impersonality, of figures to the confusion, agitation, and vagueness of the finest prose' (*ND* 40). Her interest in science subverts traditional expectations of women's interests; and Katharine's pleasure in the rational is used subversively throughout *Night and Day*, most effectively in love scenes. When Ralph Denham, who is partially modelled on Leonard Woolf, proposes to Katharine, he is described in traditionally feminine terms as 'a person who feels', whereas his intended is almost oblivious to him, 'no more listening . . . than she was counting paving stones at her feet'. The source of her happiness is intellectual rather than amatory: 'She was feeling happier than she had felt in her life. If Denham could have seen how visibly books of algebraic symbols, pages all speckled with dots and dashes and twisted bars came before her eyes as they trod the Embankment, his secret joy in her attention might have been dispersed' (*ND* 316–17). Katharine is developing an alternative rational, algebraic language at the same time as she coolly participates in the discourse of traditional courtship.

There is also a subtext of lesbian eroticism in *Night and Day*, evident in a poignant exchange between Katharine and Mary. At the moment when Mary tells Katharine that she is not going to marry Ralph, 'her hand went down to the hem of Katharine's skirt, and fingering a line of fur, she bent her head to examine it'. As she acknowledges that Ralph '"cares for someone else"', Mary's 'head still remained bent, and her hand still rested upon her skirt' (*ND* 289). The absent Ralph is the triangulating point in the two women's sensual moment, whereas at the close of the novel the light at Mary's window triangulates the union of Ralph and Katharine: 'It burnt itself into their minds' (*ND* 535). Like Evelyn Murgatroyd in *The Voyage Out*, Mary remains single at the close of the novel, pursuing the causes of feminism and socialism. Katharine is depicted, in the closing lines, standing 'upon the threshold' of her house, poised between Ralph and an illuminated interior suggesting conformity to the ending of the traditional romantic comedy, 'burning its lamps either in expectation of them or because Rodney was still there talking to Cassandra'. And the novel closes with a sense of chiaroscuro: 'Katharine pushed the door half open . . . the light lay in soft golden grains upon the deep obscurity of the hushed and sleeping household' (*ND* 538) as the lovers part. A feminine sense of fertility is imparted by the light's 'soft golden grains', contrasting with the colder light of the stars that informs Katharine's intellectual life. A subtle exploration of gender and light tropes is going on in this novel. Woolf abandoned the conservative style of *Night and Day* for a more radical experimentalism in the novels that came after, but this threshold motif, and the stylised attention to light and shadow, remained central in her writing.

By 1932 Woolf had come to think of *Night and Day* as 'dead' (*WD* 184). She records on its publication that her friend E. M. Forster found it 'strictly formal and classical', and a disappointment after *The Voyage Out* (*D1* 310, 307–8). The *Times Literary Supplement* explained that '*Night and Day* is only a love story. It leaves politics, and war, and sociology and things like that, alone' (*CH* 76). The apparently limited scope and old-fashioned style of the novel were noted by Katherine Mansfield in her wounding review for the *Athenaeum*: 'We had thought this world was vanished for ever, that it was impossible to find on the great ocean of literature a ship that was unaware of what has been happening. . . . In the midst of our admiration it makes us feel old and chill: we had never thought to look upon its like again'(*CH* 82). R. M. Underhill, reviewing *Night and Day* for the New York *Bookman*, thought that 'the term realism has gathered a depressing sense', and he has clearly missed Woolf's point concerning 'the things one doesn't say', when he observes that 'the half expressed thought, the interrupted sentences by which the action of *Night and Day* proceeds, are baffling' (*CH* 86). The novel's engagement with the gender and hierarchy of traditional dualisms and oppositions has encouraged critics to read it in terms of Woolf's theory of androgyny, as set out in *A Room of One's Own*; and more recently, the imperial subtexts of *Night and Day* have been pointed up. Some critics, too, have detected subtexts that suggest that the novel does in fact address politics and war, albeit elliptically.

Suggested further reading

Jane Marcus, 'Enchanted Organ, Magic Bells: *Night and Day* as Comic Opera', in Marcus, *Virginia Woolf and the Languages of Patriarchy* (Bloomington: Indiana University Press, 1987)

Michael Whitworth, 'Simultaneity: A Return Ticket to Waterloo', in Whitworth, *Einstein's Wake: Relativity, Metaphor, and Modernist Literature* (Oxford: Oxford University Press, 2001)

Helen Wussow, 'Conflict of Language in Virginia Woolf's *Night and Day*', *Journal of Modern Literature* 16.1 (Summer 1989), pp. 61–73

Andrea P. Zemgulys, ' "Night and Day Is Dead": Virginia Woolf in London "Literary and Historic" ', *Twentieth Century Literature* 46.1 (2000 Spring), pp. 56–77

Jacob's Room (1922)

Jacob's Room was the first of Woolf's novels to be published by the Hogarth Press, and to have a dustwrapper designed by Vanessa Bell. Woolf considered *Jacob's Room* to be a turning point in her development as an author. 'There's no doubt in my mind', she wrote on its publication, 'that I have found out how to begin (at 40) to say something in my own voice' (*D2* 186). Critically acclaimed as Woolf's first high modernist novel, *Jacob's Room* is an avant-garde Bildungsroman, charting the life of Jacob Flanders, a privileged and educated young man, who, as his surname (echoing, too, John McCrae's poem 1915 'In Flanders Field') suggests, dies before his time in the Great War like so many of his generation. The tightly constructed, self-reflexive, narrative draws Jacob largely as an absence in the lives of others. As the title indicates, the novel addresses the social and political space that Jacob occupies, and the gap he leaves behind in death.

Divided into fourteen numbered sections, this short novel is teeming with characters touching upon Jacob's life. There are well over 150 named people in *Jacob's Room*; and characters are given in light impressionistic sketches. Occasionally the free-indirect narrative (a modernist technique that moves between third- and first-person narrative, stretching third-person voice to encompass first-person experience and voice) enters Jacob's thoughts, but mostly he is apprehended through narrative that explores the consciousness of others as they encounter him. Some encounters are head on, others are passing or elliptical. His life is given as a montage of moments rather than coherent narrative progression. Jacob is seen in many contexts, including with family and friends, at university, visiting people, in a brothel, on a trip to Greece, and so on. The novel critiques imperial patriarchal culture at the same time as it explores the construction of subjectivity. It speaks movingly to the lacunae left by the war dead, but also raises the problem of gender, class and subjectivity in the context of the postwar extension of the franchise to working-class men and partial enfranchisement of women. Will the working classes and women fill Jacob's shoes? Can women occupy the same subjective space as men, or must identity, and narratives of identity, be reinvented to accommodate the feminine? Such questions are raised by the novel's own closing question uttered by Jacob's mother to his friend as she 'held out a pair of Jacob's old shoes': '"What am I to do with these, Mr Bonamy?"' (*JR* 176).

'What I'm doing', Woolf felt during the novel's composition, 'is probably being better done by Mr Joyce' (*D2* 69). *Jacob's Room* was published in the same year as Joyce's *Ulysses*, which Woolf had already encountered in serialised form and had written about in her essay 'Modern Novels' (1919). She revised this essay for publication in 1925 as 'Modern Fiction', and it is a seminal essay on modernist technique in which she examines Joyce's technique in particular. The writing of *Jacob's Room* coincides, then, with her critical conception of a new fictional methodology. Her friend T. S. Eliot's poem *The Waste Land* was also published in 1922, and Woolf's novel, like this poem, may also be understood as a self-conscious elegy, similarly preoccupied with the limitations of its own form. As well as mourning the dead of the Great War, Woolf's novel may also in part be an elegy on her brother Thoby who died of fever in 1906, and whose privileged education and travels closely resembled those experienced by Jacob. Indeed, in her composition notes she transcribed lines in Latin from the Roman poet Catullus's ode to his dead brother. Woolf's rhythmic and repetitious prose is elegiac; and the novel has a poignant refrain on absence: 'Listless is the air in an empty room' (*JR* 39, 176). Within each numbered section, Woolf has organised her paragraphs with noticeable blank spaces between them at certain points, so that snatches of dialogue or fragmentary scenes loom up at the reader from the white surround.

Jacob's Room opens with a beach scene from Jacob's childhood in which two tropes of creativity are introduced. As Jacob plays, his widowed mother is writing a 'tear-stained' letter and Charles Steele is painting a picture whose composition is disrupted by Mrs Flanders's sudden agitation: 'Here was that woman moving – actually going to get up – confound her! He struck the

canvas a hasty violet-black dab. For the landscape needed it. It was too pale'
(*JR* 7). Jacob is depicted elusively – '"Where *is* that tiresome little boy"') –
somewhere between the 'horrid blot' on his mother's letter and the 'violet-
black dab' of Steele's painting (*JR* 7). The compositional necessity of the dab
opens up the question of how the novel itself is composed, caught between the
formal demands of art and the realist ones of life. Just as *The Voyage Out* and
Night and Day address silence and the unspoken, so *Jacob's Room* focuses on
absence. As his surname suggests, Jacob Flanders is probably already absent
from the novel, even as his presence and his subjectivity are being represented.
Jacob himself is compared to a classical Greek work of art, the zenith of
'civilisation', when his married admirer, Sandra Wentworth Williams, in a
typically fugitive glimpse of Jacob, 'got [his] head exactly on a level with the
head of the Hermes of Praxiteles. The comparison was all in his favour. But
before she could say a single word he had gone out of the Museum and left
her' (*JR* 236–7). Such classical vignettes and Jacob's sojourn in Greece echo
some of the Italian scenes in E . M. Forster's *A Room With a View* (1908).

The novel does, however, allow glimpses into Jacob's interior, something
that is often overlooked in the generalisations made by some critics. For
example, Jacob's cruel thoughts, as a young student, on the presence of
women in King's College Chapel: 'why allow women to take part in it? . . .
Heaven knows why it is. For one thing, thought Jacob, they're as ugly as sin'
(*JR* 49–50). Later, he is seen to conclude that 'women . . . are just the same as
men' (*JR* 127), but this isolated thought on equality is outweighed by his
numerous misogynist reflections, such as on the 'horribly brainless' Florinda
(*JR* 130). The narrator of *Jacob's Room* pushes to the narrational fore in
places, and the commentary becomes highly self-conscious, at one point
buttonholing the reader to 'fill in the sketch as you like' (*JR* 155); at another
asking 'What do we seek through millions of pages? Still hopefully turning
the pages – oh, here is Jacob's room' (*JR* 158). In another comic aside, the
narrator expresses the desire for the rural, while recounting Jacob's travelling
through Italy: 'And what I should like would be to get out among the fields'
(*JR* 221). Woolf was later obliged to explain that the 'opinions of the writer of
Jacobs Room . . . are not *my* opinions' (*L2* 592).

There is certainly a satiric edge to the narration: the description of the
domed library in the British Museum as 'an enormous mind', for example,
where one will encounter Plato 'cheek by jowl with Aristotle; and Shakespeare
with Marlowe' (*JR* 176), suggests an acid critique on the intellectual legacies
of patriarchy. Woolf's narrator makes sport with the linear models of Enlightenment education and autodidacticism: 'This great mind is hoarded beyond
the power of any single mind to possess it. Nevertheless . . . one can't help

thinking how one might come with a notebook, sit at a desk, and read it all through' (*JR* 176). The education available in the sacred domed library underpins the privileges of Empire enjoyed by Jacob and his peers. Thoughts on Plato in the British museum lead to the cries of a woman 'come home drunk ... "Let me in! Let me in!"' (*JR* 178), a fleeting symbol of women's exclusion from the patriarchal spaces that Jacob enjoys as an entitlement.

Lytton Strachey thought *Jacob's Room* 'astonishing' and claims that he 'occasionally almost screamed with joy at the writing' (*CH* 93). The *Times Literary Supplement* reviewer reflects positively on the 'stream of incidents, persons, and their momentary thoughts and feelings' that Woolf decants 'into little vials of crystal vividness', and on 'the delicious humour which infects every page', but is troubled that this technique 'does not create persons and characters as we secretly desire to know them' (*CH* 96–7). It is this very sketchiness of character in process that appeals to more recent readers of Woolf, influenced by French feminist theory. Meanwhile, Woolf herself attacked traditional approaches to character in 'Modern Fiction' and 'Mr Bennett and Mrs Brown' (1924). Indeed, the latter is in its first conception (1923) a riposte to Arnold Bennett's review of *Jacob's Room* for *Cassell's Weekly*, where he admires this 'exquisitely written' novel, but finds that its 'characters do not vitally survive in the mind because the author has been obsessed by details of originality and cleverness' (*CH* 113).

Suggested further reading

Edward L. Bishop, 'Mind the Gap: The Spaces in *Jacob's Room*', *Woolf Studies Annual* 10 (2004), pp. 31–49

Kathleen Dobie, 'This Is the Room That Class Built: The Structures of Sex and Class in *Jacob's Room*', in Jane Marcus (ed.), *Woolf and Bloomsbury: A Centenary Celebration* (Basingstoke: Macmillan, 1987)

Vara S. Neverow, 'The Return of the Great Goddess: Immortal Virginity, Sexual Autonomy and Lesbian Possibility in *Jacob's Room*', *Woolf Studies Annual* 10 (2004), pp. 203–32

Alex Zwerdling, '*Jacob's Room*: Woolf's Satiric Elegy', *Journal of English Literary History* 48.4 (1981 Winter), pp. 894–913

Mrs Dalloway (1925)

Mrs Dalloway remains one of Woolf's most well-read and popular novels. As the name of the eponymous heroine suggests, women's identity is considered here as circumscribed by men. Mr and Mrs Dalloway played cameo roles in Woolf's first novel, *The Voyage Out*, where they come aboard ship for part of the heroine's journey. In *Mrs Dalloway*, Clarissa Dalloway occupies centre stage. The novel appears a seamless account (there are no chapters, but there are twelve sections separated by spacing) of one June day in London in 1923, charting the parallel experiences of two figures, Clarissa Dalloway, society hostess and politician's wife, and Septimus Warren Smith, a shell-shocked young war veteran. In keeping with Woolf's theory of 'androgyny' (see *A Room of One's Own*), a double narrative unfolds in which we follow both Clarissa, haunted by a refrain from Shakespeare's *Cymbeline* ('fear no more the heat o' the sun') during preparations for her party, to be attended by various friends from her past as well as the prime minister, and Septimus in his mental decline towards suicide in the company of his despairing wife Rezia. Clarissa's sexuality is a point of considerable critical interest. She is visited by an old suitor, Peter Walsh, who has returned from India, and whom she remembers for interrupting 'the most exquisite moment of her whole life' (*MD* 52), when the friend she was in love with, Sally Seton, kissed her. This sympathetically drawn 'Sapphic' moment contrasts with Woolf's rather crude portrayal of the lesbian Doris Kilman, tutor to Clarissa's daughter.

Mrs Dalloway began life as a short story, 'Mrs Dalloway in Bond Street' (published in the *Dial* in 1923), and was drafted under the working title 'The Hours'. Woolf's ambition for this work was 'to give life & death, sanity & insanity; I want to criticise the social system, and to show it at work, at its most intense' (*D2* 248). During its writing, Woolf conceived of her method as a 'tunnelling process' (*D2* 272) whereby she 'dig[s] out beautiful caves behind my characters' with the idea that 'the caves shall connect, & each comes to daylight at the present moment' (*D2* 263). Woolf's narrative methods are subtle and elliptical, and shift between the two parallel strands, using a number of the day's passing events held in common as points of transition between them. Her free-indirect technique allows the narrative subtly to shift interior focus between characters, creating a collective discursive continuum. The structural parallels with James Joyce's *Ulysses* (1922) (similarly set on one June day, in Dublin, 1916), have encouraged critics (erroneously) to liken this method of shifting and collective free-indirect discourse in *Mrs Dalloway* to Joyce's 'stream-of-consciousness'. The sound of a car backfiring, a sky-writing plane, the song of a flowerseller and the striking of Big Ben are among the novel's points of transition between different consciousnesses.

Here is how the narrative first moves from Mrs Dalloway to Septimus Warren Smith, for example: Mrs Dalloway is in Miss Pym's flower shop when the car backfires, and Mrs Pym calls out while 'going to the window to look, and coming back and smiling apologetically with her hands full of sweet peas, as if those motor cars, those tyres of motor cars, were all *her* fault' (*MD* 22–3). It is difficult to know who is making the simile introduced by 'as if' – is it the narrator's or Mrs Dalloway's simile? The narrative shifts to the glimpses caught by 'passers-by' of the car itself: they 'had just time to see a face of the very greatest importance against the dove grey upholstery, before a male hand drew the blind and there was nothing to be seen except a square of dove grey' (*MD* 23). This abstract square becomes the point of speculation for 'rumours' that spread 'veil-like' concerning the identity of the face; and then a certain Edgar J. Watkiss is heard to proclaim '"The Proime Minister's kyar."' Attention now turns to Septimus Warren Smith 'who himself unable to pass, heard him' (*MD* 24). The prime minister will appear later at Mrs Dalloway's party.

But the narrative not only ranges spatially and subjectively, from consciousness to consciousness, it also ranges back and forth through time. And in Mrs Dalloway's consciousness, it arabesques around the remembered moment of passion between herself and Sally Seton, now also married. Mrs Dalloway remembers the kiss as a Sapphic island in a sea of patriarchy, where 'Papa' has been talking, and 'Peter Walsh and Joseph Breitkopf went on about Wagner' (*MD* 55). And it is in this context of young men of the Empire discussing opera that there

> came the most exquisite moment of her whole life passing a stone urn with flowers in it. Sally stopped; picked a flower; kissed her on the lips. The whole world might have turned upside down! The others disappeared; there she was alone with Sally. And she felt that she had been given a present, wrapped up, and told just to keep it, not to look at it – a diamond, something infinitely precious, wrapped up, which, as they walked (up and down, up and down), she uncovered, or the radiance burnt through, the revelation, the religious feeling! (*MD* 55)

The diamond becomes a symbol of a lost lesbian erotics, and the image is reprised throughout the novel.

The original erotic encounter is disrupted by the intruding return of patriarchal discourse:

> – when old Joseph and Peter faced them:
>   'Star-gazing?' said Peter.
>   It was like running one's face against a granite wall in the darkness! It was shocking; it was horrible! (*MD* 55)

Later, when Mrs Dalloway is in front of the mirror, she narcissistically defines herself as diamond-like:

> pointed; dartlike; definite. That was her self when some effort, some call
> on her to be her self, drew the parts together, she alone knew how
> different, how incompatible and composed so for the world only into one
> centre, one diamond, one woman who sat in her drawing-room and
> made a meeting-point, a radiancy no doubt in some dull lives, a refuge
> for the lonely to come to, perhaps; she had helped young people, who
> were grateful to her; had tried to be the same always, never showing a
> sign of all the other sides of her – faults, jealousies, vanities, suspicions,
> like this of Lady Bruton not asking her to lunch; which, she thought
> (combing her hair finally), is utterly base! Now, where was her
> dress?   (*MD* 57–8)

The diamond image serves here also as a model for Woolf's vortex-like methodology, in which Mrs Dalloway is understood in terms of the constellation of people she brings together, at her party, and more generally in her life. Such passages make it difficult to like the character, Mrs Dalloway, yet many readers are seduced, nevertheless, into reading her without irony. Similarly, her shopping expedition in Bond Street may be interpreted as a paean to capitalism, rather than a satiric critique on the detritus of Empire served up for the entertainment of one privileged woman's vanity.

Mrs Dalloway may have her name on the title, but the book is equally also about Septimus Warren Smith. The 'splendour' of Mrs Dalloway's party, after all, 'fell to the floor', as the news of Septimus's suicide disseminates:

> Oh! thought Clarissa, in the middle of my party, here's death, she
> thought. . . . She went on, into the little room where the Prime Minister
> had gone with Lady Bruton. Perhaps there was somebody there. But
> there was nobody. The chairs still kept the impress of the Prime
> Minister and Lady Bruton . . . What business had the Bradshaws to talk
> of death at her party? A young man had killed himself. And they talked
> of it at her party – the Bradshaws, talked of death. He had killed himself
> – but how?   (*MD* 276, 277)

The reader is left with the impression that the unsatisfactory personal and sexual politics of this powerful party hostess are somehow bound up with the larger political scene inhabited by unfortunate war veterans such as Septimus. An indictment of the sexual and gender politics and language of war is implicit.

An alternative inscription of women's experience, in a new language of the feminine, may be available in *Mrs Dalloway* in the prehistoric, primal syllables ('ee um fah um', and so on) uttered by the flowerseller whose voice is described as 'the voice of no age or sex, the voice of an ancient spring spouting from the earth', yet it is the voice of 'the battered woman':

As the ancient song bubbled up opposite Regent's Park Tube Station, still the earth seemed green and flowery; still, though it issued from so rude a mouth, a mere hole in the earth, muddy too, matted with root fibres and tangled grasses, still the old bubbling burbling song, soaking through the knotted roots of infinite ages, and skeletons and treasure, streamed away in rivulets over the pavement and all along the Marylebone Road, and down towards Euston, fertilising, leaving a damp stain.   (*MD* 124)

This rude mouth appears as the originating orifice of something that both predates and transcends the patriarchal imperialism inhabited by Mrs Dalloway and Septimus; a glimpse of a more positive vision.

'No, Lytton [Strachey] does not like Mrs Dalloway,' Woolf records on 18 June 1925, 'and what is odd, I like him all the better for saying so . . . He says . . . there is discordancy between the ornament (extremely beautiful) and what happens (rather ordinary – or unimportant)' (*D3* 32). Yet Strachey still called her writing 'genius' (*CH* 168). He quibbled over the character of Mrs Dalloway. The *Times Literary Supplement*, on the other hand, found this 'experimental' novel to depict characters 'with the tantalising fluidness of life itself' (*CH* 162). And it is this rendering of character in flux that has fascinated readers and critics ever since. Gerald Bullett remarked on its 'exhilarating deluge of impressions'; and J. F. Holms, reviewing for the *Calendar of Modern Letters*, thought *Mrs Dalloway* 'considerably the best book she has written', remarking that 'her transcriptions of immediate sensation have the freshness, delicacy and vitality of direct perception' (*CH* 170). E. M. Forster declared *Mrs Dalloway* Woolf's 'masterpiece', and in identifying a 'shimmering fabric of mysticism' in her rendering of London, he responds to Woolf's tunnelling process in similar terms: 'Required like most writers to choose between the surface and the depths as a basis of her operations, she chooses the surface and then burrows in as far as she can' (*CH* 175).

It fell to a later generation of critics to comment on the social satire of *Mrs Dalloway*, and even now the shimmering impressionistic surface of this text deflects readers from the cutting satirical edge not so deeply submerged as one might think. Septimus Warren Smith's mental illness has attracted many biographically based critical approaches to the novel, showing how his appalling medical treatment parallels Woolf's own. *Mrs Dalloway* has also been read with T. S. Eliot's *The Waste Land* in mind, but, like other women writers of the period, she departs from his apocalyptic dread of the 'unreal city', celebrating the urban scene of London as at times a powerful and liberating feminine space, for all that it is haunted by the spectres of war.

The mainstream Hollywood film *The Hours* has encouraged a further resurgence of interest in *Mrs Dalloway*. It offers an interesting reading of Woolf's novel in exploring the lesbian subtext as a lifeline for a married woman reader in an American suburbia of 1951, and inverting it as a celebration and measure of gay and lesbian life in the literary public sphere of New York in the year 2001. This makes interesting comparison with Vanessa Redgrave's film version of *Mrs Dalloway*, which has been criticised for emphasising heterosexual relations and eliding homosexual ones from Woolf's novel. Lesbian and gay readings have surfaced with the film *The Hours* but there are many other ways of reading *Mrs Dalloway*, too, not least as an elegy, like *Jacob's Room*, on the dead of the Great War.

Suggested further reading

Rachel Bowlby, 'Thinking Forward Through Mrs Dalloway's Daughter', in Bowlby, *Feminist Destinations and Further Essays on Virginia Woolf* (Edinburgh: Edinburgh University Press, 1997)

David Bradshaw, ' "Vanished, Like Leaves": The Military, Elegy and Italy in *Mrs Dalloway*', *Woolf Studies Annual* 8 (2002), pp. 107–26

Linden Peach, ' "National Conservatism" and "Conservative Nationalism": *Mrs Dalloway* (1925)', in Peach, *Virginia Woolf* (Basingstoke: Macmillan, 2000)

Birgit Spengler, 'Michael Cunningham Rewriting Virginia Woolf: Pragmatist *vs.* Modernist Aesthetics', *Woolf Studies Annual* 10 (2004), pp. 51–80

To the Lighthouse (1927)

Highly poetic and densely allusive, *To the Lighthouse* is a self-reflexive, feminist Künstlerroman. Woolf conceived its triadic structure as 'two blocks joined by a corridor' (*TLH* 44–5): Part One, 'The Window' is linked via Part Two, 'Time Passes', to Part Three, 'The Lighthouse'. Each part is subdivided into numbered sections varying in length. Set in a holiday house on the Hebridean island of Skye, Part One examines the domestic, sexual, political, philosophical and aesthetic tensions in the lives of Mr and Mrs Ramsay, a philosopher and his wife of renowned beauty, and their numerous children and guests, as they take their holiday one summer around 1910. It culminates in a banquet to celebrate the engagement of two guests, Paul and Minta. Part Three returns to the house during a summer after the Great War, when the certainties and pleasures of the prewar world have crumbled (along with Paul and Minta's marriage). During both summers, one of the guests, Lily Briscoe, hemmed in by patriarchal contempt for women's artistic abilities, and by Mrs Ramsay's forceful marital ideology, attempts a painting, which serves as self-reflexive reference point for the novel itself. Indeed, it closes with an account of her final visionary brushstroke in an elegiac moment of lyric consolation. Lily's rejection of Mr Ramsay's amorous approaches, combined with his children's defiance, suggests an unsettling, if not an overcoming, of (his) patriarchy.

The middle section, 'Time Passes', covers the intervening years, focusing on the object world of the house, and its environs, in decline and under repair, as a metaphor for the losses and changes in personal terms for the individuals in the novel as well as in wider social, and political terms. This highly experimental piece of writing, published separately to begin with, has been understood to reflect on the social and political upheavals occurring during the war period through the lens of further turbulence in the 1920s. Shockingly, major events, such as the death of Mrs Ramsay, the central figure in Part One, the death of her son in the war, and of her daughter in childbirth, are communicated in brief, stylised, parenthetical statements inserted into Woolf's sustained lyrical description of time passing in the house. Woolf's theory of androgyny (see *A Room of One's Own*) has been pressed into critical service for readings of this part of the novel, where the Great War's unsettling of gender politics is suggested by a cataclysmic 'down-pouring of immense darkness' (*TL* 195) in which 'not only was furniture confounded; there was scarcely anything left of body or mind by which one could say "This is he" or "This is she"' (*TL* 196). We might ask of this writing Auerbach's simple, but perceptive, question (directed at an earlier passage): 'Who is speaking in this paragraph?' Woolf has pushed free-indirect discourse to the limits in describing the forces at work in an empty house.

Woolf emphasised the lyric qualities of her fiction when she was 'making up "To the Lighthouse"', and had the 'idea that I will invent a new name for my books to supplant "novel". A new – by Virginia Woolf. But what? Elegy?' (*D3* 34). *To the Lighthouse* was conceived in part as an elegy on her dead parents, and is in some respects autobiographical: 'This is going to be fairly short: to have father's character done complete in it; & mothers; & St Ives; & childhood; & all the usual things I put in – life, death &c. But the centre is father's character, sitting in a boat, reciting We perished, each alone, while he crushes a dying mackerel' (*D3* 18–19). But it would be diminishing the novel to see its Hebridean setting simply as Cornwall transposed, the location of Woolf's childhood family holidays, or to read the eponymous lighthouse as simply Godrevy lighthouse, which was visible from the Stephens' Cornish retreat. Woolf's friend Violet Dickinson was diverted by Woolf herself from such a transposition: 'I'm so glad that you like some of the Lighthouse . . . Is it Cornwall? I'm not as sure as you are' (*L3* 389).

The novel offers by no means a realist account of its Hebridean setting, but it makes many references to Scottish texts, including, for example, David Hume's Enlightenment philosophy, Boswell's and Johnson's accounts of their tour of the Hebrides, and the story of the events of the '45 Rebellion (Prince Charlie and Flora Macdonald.) Such texts were staples of her father's library. Woolf felt, nevertheless, that in writing *To the Lighthouse* she had exorcised the ghosts of her parents (*MOB* 90). Vanessa Bell thanked her sister for her accurate portrayal of their mother, which she found 'more like her to me than anything I could have conceived as possible' (*L3* 572). Reading *To the Lighthouse* involves the reader remaining open to both the autobiographical and the fictional at the same time. 'Nothing [is] simply one thing' (*TL* 286) in this text, as one of its characters, James, concludes when in sight of the lighthouse. And *To the Lighthouse* is brimming with allusions to and citations of many other poetic and literary texts: Virgil, Shakespeare, Milton, Marvell, Tennyson, Scott and more. During Part One, Mr Ramsay charges around the garden reciting Tennyson's 'The Charge of the Light Brigade' while Mrs Ramsay is reading to her son the Grimms fairy tale 'The Fisherman and His Wife', which is a cautionary tale against an overambitious wife. At the close of Part One, she is reading Shakespeare's sonnets, while Mr Ramsay reads a novel by Scott.

The dense, self-conscious layering of metaphor and symbolism in *To the Lighthouse* requires many levels of interpretation. The reader is constantly invited to ponder how the lighthouse itself, for example, might be understood. 'I meant nothing by The Lighthouse', Woolf wrote to her friend Roger Fry, the formalist aesthete:

> One has to have a central line down the middle of the book to hold the design together. I saw that all sorts of feelings would accrue to this, but I refused to think them out, and trusted that people would make it the deposit for their own emotions. . . . I can't manage Symbolism except in this vague, generalised way. . . . Directly I'm told what a thing means, it becomes hateful to me.   (*L3* 385)

Such discussion shows how far Woolf has moved the genre of her novel towards poetry. The normal frames of reference for fiction, such as plot and character, have given way to consideration of poetic device and philosophy. Like much of its contemporary poetic elegy, too, *To the Lighthouse* speaks more generally of the dead of the Great War, and of the passing of one way of life to a radically different one, practically and philosophically, a transition made possible by the social and political changes that accompanied the war.

Mrs Ramsay represents the social adhesive of the prewar years, and her triumphant banquet, implicitly celebrating the engagement of Paul and

Minta, represents the continuity of her reactionary patriarchal family values. Mrs Ramsay is the mother and wife who likes to say yes to her son and her husband. The first word of the novel is 'Yes' and it is uttered by Mrs Ramsay, to mollify her son: ' "YES, of course, if it's fine to-morrow," said Mrs Ramsay. "But you'll have to be up with the lark," she added. To her son these words conveyed an extraordinary joy' (*TL* 11). And Mrs Ramsay says 'Yes' to her husband, too: 'Her husband was so sensible, so just. And so she said, "Yes; all children go through stages" ' (*TL* 105); 'He would like a little solitude. Yes, she said. It annoyed him that she did not protest' (*TL* 110). The closing words of Part One, 'The Window', are hers unspoken, in victorious self-subordination, to her husband: ' "Yes, you were right. It's going to be wet to-morrow." She had not said it, but he knew it. And she looked at him smiling. For she had triumphed again' (*TL* 191). Mrs Ramsay's 'Yes' is deployed as an affirmation of patriarchal matrimony at every turn. Section 15 of 'The Window', for example, comprises only one sentence, spoken by the patriarchal daughter Prue (who will die in childbirth in parentheses in 'Time Passes'): ' "Yes," said Prue, in her considering way, answering her mother's question, "I think Nancy did go with them" (*TL* 124; see also 113, 142, 163). And it is interesting to watch how 'yes' is deployed in the mouths of the surviving characters after Mrs Ramsay's death (see *TL* 228, 230).

In *To the Lighthouse* 'yes' is also sometimes followed by 'but' (see *TL* 11, 106); and after Lily Briscoe implicitly refuses the widowed Mr Ramsay's mournful advances, she finally says yes, not to a man, but to her own art, in the closing paragraph of the novel, which is rhythmically punctuated by two yeses: "There it was – her picture. Yes, with all its green and blues, its lines running up and across, its attempt at something. . . . With a sudden intensity, as if she saw it clear for a second, she drew a line there, in the centre. It was done; it was finished. Yes, she thought, laying down her brush in extreme fatigue, I have had my vision" (*TL* 319). Lily represents an alternative, creative path for women, than the marriage prospectus set out by Mrs Ramsay. The marriage of Paul and Minta founders in the third part of the novel. The unmarried, independent Lily, in many respects, 'override[s]' Mrs Ramsay's wishes at the same time as she memorialises her in her painting.

In Part One Lily is interrogated by William Bankes, one of the Ramsays' guests, about her painting technique. Just as the painting may be understood as a self-conscious analogue for the novel in which it appears, does Lily's explanation serves as the novel's implicit aesthetic manifesto. Bankes asks Lily what she wished 'to indicate by the triangular purple shape just there?' Lily explains that her abstract coloured shape is 'Mrs Ramsay reading to James . . . She knew his objection that no one could tell it for a human shape. But she had made no attempt at a likeness, she said.' Her defence makes clear that the painting, like the novel, is not a realist project. Mr Bankes ponders how 'Mother and child then – objects of universal veneration, and in this case the mother was famous for her beauty – might be reduced . . . to a purple shadow without irreverence' (*TL* 84–5). The remarks in parenthesis show how patriarchy, in the form of Mr Bankes, has already positioned Mrs Ramsay as an aesthetic object before her appearance in the painting. Lily's Post-Impressionist technique of dreaming before nature may be understood to subvert this by adopting a nonmimetic aesthetic mode of expression, one that nevertheless correlates with the shape of mother and son on the step. Mr Bankes represents the reactionary views attributed to the man in the street who is baffled by modern art. He understands art in crudely monetary and mimetic, realist terms: 'The largest picture in his drawing room, which painters had praised, and valued at a higher price than he had given for it, was of the cherry trees in blossom on the banks of the Kennet. He had spent his honeymoon on the banks of the Kennet, he said' (*TL* 85). His sentimentalism fits with the kind of greetings-card sentimentalism that Bloomsbury Post-Impressionism vehemently attacked. Lily's picture, she explains 'was not of them . . . not in his sense' (*TL* 85). In the third part of the book, Lily paints a fresh version of the same scene, except that Mrs Ramsay is absent, having died parenthetically in the middle part of the novel. Lily attempts both to represent the absent Mrs Ramsay and to overcome her absence and her influence.

Just as Mr Bankes is shocked by Lily's representation of Mrs Ramsay, so Woolf's readers may be shocked by the novel's representation of Mrs Ramsay's death: '[Mr Ramsay stumbling along a passage stretched his arms out one dark morning, but Mrs Ramsay having died rather suddenly the night before he stretched his arms out. They remained empty]' (*TL* 200). This is the low point of 'Time Passes'. There are other deaths recorded here, each in parenthesis – the fall of a son in the Great War, the loss of a daughter in the pain of giving birth. But it is the death of the novel's central character, Mrs Ramsay, so casually reported, that most shocks. The notorious stumbling sentence in which the patriarch, Mr Ramsay, reaches out for his faithful wife, only to clasp thin air, has given readers (and editors) considerable trouble (especially as the first American edition gives a substantive variant). The passage may well allude to the story of Orpheus and Eurydice, a husband losing his wife at the gates of Hell. Mr Ramsay also seems to have learnt the lesson of Andrew Marvell's *carpe diem* in 'To His Coy Mistress': 'The grave's a fine and private place,/But none, I think, do there embrace.'

As well as overriding Mrs Ramsay's wishes, Lily is seen to override Mr Ramsay's wishes and his philosophy. Mr Ramsay is satirically depicted, in the first part of *To the Lighthouse*, exercising his disciplined Enlightenment mind as if it were a 'keyboard' or an 'alphabet' (his analogy). He finds himself stumbling at Q, which comes before his own initial: 'He reached Q. Very few people in the whole of England ever reach Q . . . But after Q? What comes next? . . . Z is only reached once by one man in a generation. Still if he could reach R it would be something. Here at least was Q' (*TL* 56–7). He understands his 'splendid' mind as part of a larger order of enlightened masculine subjectivity: 'His own little light would shine, not very brightly, for a year or two, and would then be merged in some bigger light, and that in a bigger still' (*TL* 59). Lily puts forward an alternative model of intellectual endeavour by understanding enlightenment in non-linear terms as 'little daily miracles, illuminations, matches struck unexpectedly in the dark' (*TL* 249).

Mrs McNab and Mrs Bast, the cleaning ladies who appear in the middle part of the novel, may also be understood as putting forward another model for women's subjectivity. They labour to rescue the neglected summerhouse from disrepair:

> Slowly and painfully, with broom and pail, mopping, scouring,
> Mrs McNab, Mrs Bast stayed the corruption and the rot; rescued from
> the pool of Time that was fast closing over them now a basin, now a
> cupboard; fetched from oblivion all the Waverley novels and a tea-set
> one morning; in the afternoon restored to sun and air a brass fender
> and a set of tool irons. (*TL* 215)

Woolf's rendering here of working-class women as chthonic goddesses, conferring life and fertility in the midst of decay, may also be understood as a political allegory describing the social transformations that occurred during and after the Great War.

The commercial success of *To the Lighthouse* was sufficient for Woolf to purchase a car on her proceeds, and the novel met with serious critical interest. The *Times Literary Supplement* found it as 'elastic as a novel can be', but was doubtful over the achievement of the middle part (*CH* 193–4). Rachel Taylor, reviewing for the *Spectator*, on the other hand, admired how 'Time Passes' 'in some passages chants heavily and dreamily like the prose litanies of Mallarmé' (*CH* 199). The poet Edwin Muir, reviewing for the *Nation and Athenaeum*, enjoyed 'Time Passes' as work by 'a writer of profound imagination', but worried that 'how this kind of imagination can be applied, as one feels sure it can, to the business of the novelist, the shadowing forth of human life, is still a problem to be solved' (*CH* 209–210). Arnold

Bennett, one of Woolf's harshest critics, was baffled not by Woolf's rendering of character, but by her slender plot. 'The scheme of the story is rather wilful', he opined, '– designed seemingly, but perhaps not really, to exhibit virtuosity. A group of people plan to sail in a small boat to a lighthouse. At the end some of them reach the lighthouse in a small boat. That is the externality of the plot' (*CH* 200). Bennett is merely highlighting what generations of readers of *To the Lighthouse* discover with more pleasure than he – that they are reading a novel not for any of the conventional expectations of plot or character, but for its ability to compress in its narrative all the lyric achievements of poetry, while simultaneously performing the work of prose in recounting profound historical changes.

To the Lighthouse is one of the most widely read and critically scrutinised of Woolf's novels and has been examined in relation to every modern phase of literary criticism from formalism to postmodernism and postcolonialism. Her early formulations of the work as an elegy on her parents led many later critics to understand the novel as 'frankly biographical'. On the other hand, the aesthetic formalism of *To the Lighthouse* has also engaged a deal of formalist criticism. There have been numerous readings of the novel and its imagery as enigmatic, mystical and nebulously symbolic. The novel's playfulness with typographical presentation (its famous brackets, in particular) prompt one to ask how such a novel as *To the Lighthouse* might ever be successfully translated to the medium of film, without losing its important qualities as written text. (There has been one unsatisfactory television version, for example.) We might also consider the attempts of various critics and writers to describe and even produce visual art that might be said to embody the aesthetic of Lily Briscoe's painting, or indeed to reproduce it (the work of the Australian artist Suzanne Bellamy is particularly interesting in this respect).

Suggested further reading

Erich Auerbach, 'The Brown Stocking' (1946), in Rachel Bowlby (ed.), *Virginia Woolf* (London: Longman, 1992)

Gillian Beer, 'Hume, Stephen, and Elegy in *To the Lighthouse*', in Beer, *Virginia Woolf: The Common Ground* (Edinburgh: Edinburgh University Press, 1996)

Suzanne Bellamy, Artist's Statement and art work: http://home.goulburn.net.au/~sbellamy/

Rachel Bowlby 'Getting to Q: Sexual Lines in To the Lighthouse', in Bowlby, *Feminist Destinations and Further Essays on Virginia Woolf* (Edinburgh: Edinburgh University Press, 1997)

Janet Winston, ' "Something Out of Harmony": *To the Lighthouse* and the Subject(s) of Empire', *Woolf Studies Annual* 2 (1996), pp. 39–70

Orlando: A Biography (1928)

Orlando is considered 'the longest and most charming love letter in literature', and is dedicated to Woolf's lover Vita Sackville-West. Woolf conceived of it as 'an escapade after these serious poetic experimental books'. She wanted 'the main note' of this mock biography to be 'Satire'; '– satire and wildness'. And the target of the satire is to include her 'own lyric vein' (*D3* 131). 'Half laughing, half serious; with great splashes of exaggeration' (*D3* 168), the novel tells the story of Orlando, perennial heir to Knole, the Sackville stately home, who at the start of the book is a young nobleman and aspiring poet of the Elizabethan period and by the close, after a few hundred years of literary, amorous and heroic adventures and encounters with nearly all the great literary canonical figures through the ages, is married, and a successful *woman* poet. Her poem 'The Oak Tree', hundreds of years in gestation, wins a literary prize and critical acclaim. As well as a spoof biography, then, *Orlando* may also be seen as a satirical Künstlerroman, exploring the gender politics of poetics and artistic subjectivity across the ages.

Orlando changes sex in the middle of the novel during a tour of duty as Charles II's ambassador to Constantinople, but also further complicates gender expectations when as a man he masquerades as a woman, and as a woman masquerades as a man. This mock biography perhaps also takes a swipe at other Bloomsbury biographical innovators such as Lytton Strachey and Vita's husband, Harold Nicolson, in a review of whose work Woolf coined her famous phrase, 'granite and rainbow'. *Orlando* is written in six chapters and mockingly sports a preface, illustrations (including elaborately staged photographs) and an index. In spite of all these trimmings, there is still a strong sense that the character Orlando is a portrait of Vita Sackville-West: 'Suppose Orlando turns out to be Vita,' Woolf wrote to her, 'and its all about you and the lusts of your flesh and the lure of your mind' (*L3* 428). This is a new form of biography; and Woolf boasted that she 'could revolutionise biography in a night' (*L3* 429).

Planning *Orlando*, but already with her later work *The Waves* in mind, Woolf thought it would 'be great fun to write; & it will rest my head before starting the very serious, mystical poetical work which I want to come next' (*D3* 131). But as well as being a pleasurable diversion, she also conceived of *Orlando* as a new form of memoir and biography: 'One of these days . . . I shall sketch here, like a grand historical picture the outlines of all my friends. . . . It might be a way of writing the memoirs of one's own times during peoples lifetimes' (*D3* 156–7). Again, the reader of *Orlando* is put on

treacherous ground, between granite and rainbow, between recognising portraits of real people at the same time as acknowledging the licence of fiction.
Woolf herself understood the challenge of writing this work to be that of
carefully balancing 'between truth & fantasy' (*D3* 162). On its completion,
she found that writing *Orlando* had taught her 'how to write a direct
sentence; taught me continuity & narrative, & how to keep the realities at
bay. But I purposely avoided of course any other difficulty. I never got down
to my depths & made shapes square up, as I did in The Lighthouse' (*D3* 203).
This seems to suggest a certain facile lightness of touch in *Orlando*; and
Woolf even records feeling bored as she writes the closing chapter: 'One gets
bored. One whips oneself up. I still hope for a fresh wind, & don't very much
bother' (*D3* 175). Indeed, the reader may well sense the narrative's flagging
towards the close of the novel, after an explosive and virtuoso first half.

   Orlando, which owes a great deal to the Italian Renaissance poem *Orlando
Furioso* (1532) by Ariosto, opens in Elizabethan times, with the hero in male
form and 'in the act of slicing at the head of a Moor which swung from the
rafters'. In this he embodies the enterprising colonial impulse of Elizabethan
culture and he is duly rewarded by the Queen herself. The arrival of
Elizabeth, who so famously transcended her gender as powerful sovereign,
to bestow the property of Knole upon his family, is communicated in an
erotic description of the landscape that Orlando has dominion over for the
hundreds of years the novel goes on to chart. His view of the landscape seems
to bring luminous colour to the previously 'dark country' of feminine
sexuality: 'the sun was rapidly sinking, the white clouds had turned red, the
hills were violet, the woods purple, the valleys black – a trumpet sounded.
Orlando leapt to his feet. The shrill sound came from the valley.' The trumpet
sound seems to herald an intimate sense of feminine sexuality: ' It came from
a dark spot down there; a spot compact and mapped out; a maze; a town, yet
girt with walls; it came from the heart of his own great house in the valley,
which, dark before, even as he looked and the single trumpet duplicated and
reduplicated itself with other shriller sounds, lost its darkness and became
pierced with lights' (*O* 21).

   At the time when day meets night, a man (who later becomes a woman)
looks down upon a valley in the dying sunlight. As the sun goes down, each
item seen is described as a darker colour than the last – from 'white clouds' to
'valleys black', in shades of red. When blackness is reached instead of noth-
ingness or amorphous obscurity, a trumpet call heralds a new landscape, in
which is discerned a 'dark spot'; and as eyes adjust, what once was described
as 'darkness' is now 'pierced with lights'. The subversiveness of this vision

is replicated by the discovery by this man (who is to become a woman) of 'his own great house in the valley'. This vision of a liberated feminine sexuality is accompanied by a 'fanfare', the 'shrill sound' of the 'trumpet', marking feminine pleasure, culminating in a fairly explicit suggestion of orgasm: 'Coaches turned and wheeled in the courtyard. Horses tossed their plumes. The Queen had come' (*O* 21). That this trumpet sound is a coded reference to feminine sexual pleasure is confirmed at the key turning point in the novel where Orlando undergoes his change of sex, a transition likewise accompanied by a fanfare of trumpets: 'The trumpeters, ranging themselves side by side in order, blow one terrific blast', and at the 'trumpets pealed Truth! Truth! Truth! we have no choice left but confess – he was a woman' (*O* 126). Five asterisks then mark this bifurcating point in the novel. In everything that precedes, Orlando is a man; in everything that follows, a woman. 'A Queen' and a 'wild goose' are the portents at the close of the novel, which sees Orlando married to Shelmerdine, whom she meets in the nineteenth century and is 'now grown a fine sea captain'. Its closing words record the date of *Orlando*'s publication: 'midnight, Thursday, the eleventh of October, Nineteen hundred and Twenty Eight' (*O* 295).

Reading *Orlando* can be a disorienting experience, as the text brings together such diverse elements. The scene where the Great Frost of Tudor times melts leaving various parties stranded on ice floes on the Thames may serve as an analogue for the text: 'For furniture, valuables, possessions of all sorts were carried away on the icebergs. Among other strange sights was to be seen a cat suckling its young; a table laid sumptuously for a supper of twenty; a couple in bed; together with an extraordinary number of cooking utensils.' And his reader may well identify with Orlando's experience, as 'dazed and astounded, [he] could do nothing for some time but watch the appalling race of waters as it hurled itself past him' (*O* 60).

As well as presenting to the reader a procession of famous writers, including Shakespeare, Marlowe, Jonson, Dryden, Pope, Johnson and Boswell, the novel also indulges in purple passages describing *Orlando*'s changing landscapes, and interiors, with special focus on Knole itself, the stately home of the Sackville-Wests. Towards the close Orlando seeks out the 'heart of the house', the Ambassador's bedroom, a sumptuous room with an enormous matrimonial bed, in which she watches 'the tapestry rising and falling on the eternal faint breeze which never failed to move it. Still the hunter rode; still Daphne flew. The heart still beat, she thought, however faintly, however far withdrawn; the frail indomitable heart of the immense building' (*O* 285). This is presumably where generations of Sackville-Wests have been conceived. Satirised here is the sentimental sense of familial continuity in the house, one that masks a dark undertow of misogyny, as supplied by the allusion to the myth of Daphne fleeing rape by Apollo.

Woolf explores in *Orlando* how different contexts, including spatial as well as temporal contexts, require different selves. Orlando is described in the process of self-fashioning, of mustering the right self for the occasion, a process Woolf elucidates in one of her stunningly elastic, elongated sentences:

> Orlando? Still the Orlando she needs may not come; these selves of which we are built up, one on top of another, as plates are piled on a waiter's hand, have attachments elsewhere, sympathies, little constitutions and rights of their own, call them what you will (and for many of these things there is no name) so that one will only come if it is raining, another when Mrs Jones is not there, another if you can promise it a glass of red wine – and so on; for everybody can multiply from his own experience the different terms which his different selves have made with him – and some are too wildly ridiculous to be mentioned in print at all.   (*O* 277)

This sentence allows modern understanding of subjectivity as something multiple and in process, something shaped by material circumstance and social constellation. Orlando's fluctuating between genders, evident in her transition from male to female, and his and her cross-dressing, may be understood to fulfil Woolf's theory of androgyny (see *A Room of One's Own*). On the other hand, it might be argued that such masquerading actually serves elliptically to celebrate lesbian identity, rather than destabilising sexual identity altogether.

On first reading *Orlando*, its dedicatee Vita Sackville-West discovered a 'new form of Narcissism' by falling in love with Orlando (*L3* 574). Arnold Bennett thought *Orlando* 'a high-brow lark' (*CH* 232) while Rebecca West deemed it 'a poetic masterpiece'. Evading the censorship that Radclyffe Hall's notorious lesbian novel, *The Well of Loneliness* (1928), met with in the same period, *Orlando* has since attracted many readings concerned with Woolf's theories of androgyny and, latterly, lesbian aesthetics. There is a popular film version of *Orlando* (1992), directed by Sally Potter and starring Tilda Swinton, that does justice to Woolf's playful interrogation of gender roles, with sumptuous period sets and costumes, and takes Orlando's story into the 1990s.

Suggested further reading

Rachel Bowlby, 'Orlando's Undoing', in Bowlby, *Feminist Destinations and Further Essays on Virginia Woolf* (Edinburgh: Edinburgh University Press, 1997)

Catherine Craft-Fairchild, ' "Same Person . . . Just a Different Sex": Sally Potter's Construction of Gender in *Orlando*', *Woolf Studies Annual* 7 (2001), pp. 23–48
Jane de Gay, ' "Though the Fashion of the Time Did Something to Disguise It": Staging Gender in Woolf's *Orlando*', in Jessica Berman and Jane Goldman (eds.), *Virginia Woolf Out of Bounds: Selected Papers from the Tenth Annual Conference on Virginia Woolf* (New York: Pace University Press, 2001)
Suzanne Raitt, *Vita & Virginia: The Work and Friendship of Vita Sackville-West and Virginia Woolf* (Oxford: Clarendon, 1993)

The Waves (1931)

The Waves is considered Woolf's most difficult, high modernist text. It is a beautifully stylised, poetical work that alternates descriptive pastoral passages with sets of soliloquies by six characters. After the first pastoral interlude, describing sunrise on a seascape, the reader is plunged into the orchestrated voices of the characters in childhood. The language is pleasingly poetic and prompts comparative thoughts of childhood in the reader. This opening seems to touch people of all backgrounds, because it is written in such a way as to encourage the reader to participate in the narrative with his/her own recollections. Woolf conceived *The Waves* as 'a new kind of play . . . prose yet poetry; a novel & a play' (*D3* 128), and it is certainly difficult to categorise. It comprises nine italicised pastoral interludes, describing the diurnal progress of the sun across a seascape and landscape, interwoven with nine multivocal sections of interrelated soliloquies by Bernard, Jinny, Louis, Neville, Rhoda and Susan, from childhood to maturity. Percival, a seventh character, who dies in youth, is the voiceless centre of their circle. Rhoda, the most alienated of the group commits suicide, a fact communicated in the last soliloquy, Bernard's final summing up. *The Waves* is, then, an elegy on Percival and Rhoda, with wider elegiac resonances. Woolf was tempted, for example, to write her dead brother Thoby's name on the final page of the manuscript. The text is dense with literary allusions and the three male speakers are all aspiring writers of sorts; it is thus in a sense a Künstlerroman.

The interludes closely describe the play of light, shadow and colours during the sun's progress across the sky in terms that suggest a politics of gender. The first interlude, often compared with Genesis, describes dawn bringing division into a world previously without light: '*The sun had not yet risen. The sea was indistinguishable from the sky.*' The '*woman couched beneath the horizon . . . rais[ing] a lamp*' (*W* 5) suggests both woman as enslaved functionary of the patriarchal order, and woman as appropriating the icon of masculine subjectivity (the sun). After this primal scene, in the first section of soliloquies, the six characters begin imaginatively to explore their world in pastoral terms. Louis, for example, 'left standing by the wall among the flowers' makes them vehicles of his imagination (*W* 10); Bernard and Susan frighten themselves with sinister figures (the 'lady writing' and 'the gardeners sweeping') in their imaginary 'Elvedon' (*W* 15–16). Rhoda emerges as highly creative in this respect, developing inside an imaginary world of her own ('a short space of freedom'), unable to concentrate and integrate as well as the others. 'All my ships are white,' she declares as she creates a pastoral world in which she manipulates carefully selected objects, inventing a story about a shipwrecked sailor – a piscatory elegy perhaps (*W* 17). This first section of soliloquies describes the common and then segregated education of the two sexes, as Jinny summarises: 'We shall part. You will go to school. You will have masters wearing crosses with white ties. I shall have a mistress in a school on the East Coast who sits under a portrait of Queen Alexandra. This is where I am going, and Susan and Rhoda' (*W* 22–3). But perhaps the sense of gender division is already in place before this (as the Genesis-like scene of the first interlude suggests). The recurrent image of 'the lady writing' first seen by Bernard and Susan in 'Elvedon' (*W* 15), may, like Bernard, be understood as the author of the interludes. The other sections of soliloquies focus on the development of the characters to maturity, highlighted by two dinners, of farewell and reunion.

Woolf had a vision of the work that was to be *The Waves* while she was completing *To the Lighthouse* in the autumn of 1926, when she glimpsed, in the midst of depression, 'a fin passing far out . . . I hazard a guess that it may be the impulse behind another book' (*D* 113). Her working title was 'The Moths', reflecting another source of inspiration in her sister Vanessa's account in a letter of huge moths that flew into her house in France. Woolf replied: 'your story of the moth so fascinates me that I am going to write a story about it. I can think of nothing else but you and the moths for hour's after reading your letter' (*L3* 372). She thought out its beginning in terms of 'dawn; the shells on a beach' and 'Childhood', adding: 'but it must not be *my* childhood' (*D3* 236). Her initial thoughts for this 'play-poem' were sketched out while listening to her 'gramophone . . . playing late Beethoven sonatas' (*D3* 139). And during its composition Woolf drew on both musical and painterly analogies in claiming to be 'writing The Waves to a rhythm not to a plot', a rhythm that 'is in harmony with the painters' (*D3* 316).

Rhythm is the structuring force of *The Waves*, but Woolf also found herself 'now & then haunted by some semi mystic very profound life of a woman, which shall be told on one occasion; & time shall be utterly obliterated; future shall somehow blossom out of the past. One incident – say the fall of a flower – might contain it' (*D3* 118). She seems to be envisaging a feminist allegory.

This early glimpse of *The Waves* is intriguing, for it seems to bear little resemblance to the novel published five years later, where Percival constitutes an absent central focus, and Bernard comes to dominate with his summing up. In retrospect, Woolf recognises her innovatory symbolic technique in *The Waves* and 'the freedom & boldness with which my imagination picked up used & tossed aside all the images & symbols', which she used 'not in set pieces . . . but simply as images; never making them work out; only suggest. Thus I hope to have kept the sound of the sea & the birds, dawn, & garden subconsciously present, doing their work under ground' (*D4* 10–11).

Rather than think of Woolf's initial idea to chart 'some semi mystic . . . life of a woman' as having disappeared by the time of the novel's completion, perhaps we might find it still present, suggested at this 'under ground' level of imagery. 'Mystic', as well as referring to sacred, obscure religious feelings, may also suggest 'a secret meaning hidden from the eyes of the ordinary person, only revealed to a spiritually enlightened mind: allegorical', according to the *Chambers Concise Dictionary* (1991). Woolf's 'semi mystic' text refers to a quasi-sacred mythology, and is partly coded and allegorical. Woolf's qualification is significant: the woman's life is to be '*semi* mystic'. A later projection suggests the novel to be about her *struggle* to 'come to terms with these mystical feelings' (*D3* 203), again suggesting a cryptic rather than mystical impulse. Woolf also expresses ambitions for a less abstract project: 'I want to write a history, say of Newnham or the womans movement in the same vein. The vein is deep in me – at least sparkling, urgent' (*D3* 203). These feminist aspirations, though addressed in *A Room of One's Own*, may extend to *The Waves*.

Woolf's organisation of *The Waves* into subjective passages by the six soliloquists, punctuated by objective pastoral passages without a marked narrator, suggests a concern both with subjectivity (individual and collective) and phenomenology, with subjective engagement and objective detachment, with processes of the self, as well as absence of the self. To talk of separate people in *The Waves* is perhaps, then, to miss the point: 'The six characters were supposed to be one. I'm getting old myself . . . and I come to feel more and more how difficult it is to collect oneself into one Virginia' (*L6* 397). Woolf puts forward a sense of contested, incomplete or multiple, subjectivity, which is relevant to understanding the novel's alternation between soliloquies and interludes. It is possible to see Bernard as author of the interludes, or to understand each character as participating in voicing them; but although Bernard does come to dominate, he does not, nor does any other individual speaker, recount everything that occurs in these passages. The interludes are not 'objective' phenomenological accounts of the natural world, but pastorals over whose interpretation various voices vie (including the reader's). They tell many stories, identifiable both with individual soliloquies and with narratives beyond them. The reader, then, engages in a process of interpreting the interludes both separately and in relation to the soliloquies. There are snatches of and allusions to numerous literary texts in both interludes and soliloquies, including classical mythology and Romantic poetry. Rhoda, for example, recites refrains from a number of Shelley's poems, including 'The Question', 'The Indian Serenade' and 'Arethusa' (*W* 60). This densely allusive, self-consciously poetic text suggests itself in this way as a kind of imploded Künstlerroman. Bernard, the writer, sums up, but his development as an individual writer can be understood only in terms of the position of his voice in a colloquy of those of his peers.

All three male speakers develop openly literary ambitions, taking themselves seriously as writers, authors in the world. Bernard thinks of himself as Byron (*W* 89); Louis thinks himself 'the companion of Plato, of Virgil' (*W* 102); Neville adores Catullus and fantasises that he will 'addict [himself] to perfection; to follow the curve of the sentence wherever it might lead, into deserts, under drifts of sand, regardless of lures, of seductions; to be poor always and unkempt; to be ridiculous in Picadilly' (*W* 94). But the three women function at a different level of self-knowledge and social expectation. Susan and Jinny are rural and urban versions of women subordinated to the male order. Susan is a mother figure aligned with nature, who nevertheless has moments when she wonders 'But who am I, who lean on this gate . . .? I think sometimes (I am not twenty yet) I am not a woman . . . I am the seasons, I think sometimes, January, May, November; the mud, the mist, the dawn' (*W* 105). Jinny is promiscuous and metropolitan, and self-consciously and a little uncomfortably an object for erotic contemplation: 'I feel myself shining in the dark. Silk is on my knee. My silk legs rub smoothly together. The stones of a necklace lie cold on my throat. My feet feel the pinch of shoes. I sit bolt upright so that my hair may not touch the back of the seat. I am arrayed, I am prepared' (*W* 109). Rhoda does not fit in socially or sexually, yet nor does she fight for her place: 'I am thrust back to stand burning in this clumsy, this ill-fitting body, to receive the shafts of his indifference and his scorn, I who long for marble columns and pools on the other side of the world where the swallow dips her wings' (*W* 113). She does not successfully intervene in the material world but more and more retreats from its indifference. Her visions are cryptic spaces that become increasingly remote, abstract and enclosed.

At the dinner party in honour of Percival, the unvoiced Percival acts as the focal point of the other six selves. Rhoda is warmed by the incidental 'general blaze' of the group who gather round him (*W* 142). Jinny describes the socially connective '[m]embranes, webs of nerves that lay white and limp,' veiling the dinner-table discourse from the material world beyond. Louis notes that 'The roar of London . . . is round us' (*W* 146), and Neville that 'lit up' and 'many coloured', 'we are walled in here. But India lies outside' (*W* 147). The diners, then, inhabit a luminous, yet slightly dingy, imperialist halo, outside which lies the subject nation, India, for which their solar hero is destined. From this dank cocoon Bernard projects his vision of Percival as imperial overlord 'applying the standards of the West' (*W* 147). The reader is left to contemplate the complicity of the entire group in the processes of Empire. When Percival dies, in an elegiac moment of lyric consolation Rhoda scatters violets for him on the water at Greenwich: 'Now I will relinquish; now I will let loose . . . We will gallop together over desert hills where the swallow dips her wings in dark pools and the pillars stand entire. Into the wave that dashes upon the shore, into the wave that flings its white foam to the uttermost corners of the earth, I throw my violets to Percival' (*W* 178). This moment prefigures the final words of Bernard's summing up in which he inveighs against mortality: 'Death is my enemy. It is death against whom I ride with my spear couched and my hair flying back like a young man's, like Percival's, when he galloped in India. I strike my spurs into my horse. Against you I will fling myself, unvanquished and unyielding, O Death!' (*W* 325). Bernard's imperial simile prompts questions over the status of Empire in the novel: is it being condoned or criticised? Why does Bernard sum up? And what do we make of Rhoda's suicide, only reported elliptically by Bernard ('I see far away, quivering like a gold thread, the pillar Rhoda saw, and feel the rush of the wind of her flight when she leapt') (*W* 316)?

As well as examining the self in relation to others, *The Waves* also explores the solitary self in existential crisis. One of the most powerful episodes is Bernard's description of the sun going out on his sense of himself. In losing himself, he also seems to lose the world: 'The scene beneath me withered. It was like the eclipse when the sun went out and left the earth, flourishing in full summer foliage, withered, brittle, false. . . . The woods had vanished; the earth was a waste of shadow. . . . A man without a self, I said. A heavy body leaning on a gate. A dead man' (*W* 311, 312). This is an expression of individual masculine subjective loss, but it is simultaneously a metafictional moment in a self-conscious stylised work that seeks to test the limits of language itself: 'But how describe the world seen without a self? There are no words. Blue, red – even they distract, even they hide with thickness instead of letting the light through' (*W* 314). Bernard appears to achieve a state of androgyny when he claims: 'Nor do I always know if I am man or woman' (*W* 123). The novel, nevertheless, to some extent dissents from Bernard's imperialist attempts to 'sum up' (*W* 260) all identities. In describing the return of the self, Bernard dwells on a sense of subjective fragility as the return of the light is described:

> Miraculously. Frailly. In thin stripes. It hangs like a glass cage. It is a hoop to be fractured by a tiny jar. There is a spark there. Next moment a flush of dun. Then a vapour as if the earth were breathing in and out, once, twice, for the first time. Then under the dullness someone walks with a green light. Then off twists a white wraith. The woods throb blue and green, and gradually the fields drink in red, gold, brown. Suddenly a river snatches a blue light. The earth absorbs colour like a sponge slowly drinking water. It puts on weight; rounds itself; hangs pendent; settles and swings beneath our feet.   (*W* 313)

This passage recalls Woolf's diary account of the solar eclipse she witnessed in June 1927, an account she drew on also for her essay 'The Sun and the Fish'. It is a vulnerable and fragile world that hangs at Bernard's feet.

'No two people', according to Woolf, 'think alike about' *The Waves* (*L5* 144); and she gleefully reports that it was considered by Vita Sackville-West 'so bad that only a small dog that had been fed on gin could have written it' (*L4* 401). But Vanessa Bell found herself 'completely submerged in The Waves', and 'gasping, out of breath, choking, half-drowned . . . so overcome by the beauty' (*VB* 361). The *Times Literary Supplement* reviewer wrote of 'a glittering rain of impressions and reactions' in *The Waves*, and invoked Woolf's 'luminous halo' passage from 'Modern Fiction' to describe its poetic qualities, and its sense of 'rhythmical incantation' (*CH* 264). Harold Nicolson, reviewing for *Action*, called it 'a literary sensation' that surpasses James Joyce's handling of 'the internal monologue' (*CH* 266). G. Lowes Dickinson thought of the six soliloquists as 'six imagist poets, six facets of the imagist poet that Mrs Woolf is herself' (*CH* 275). Robert Herrick's barbed review for the New York *Saturday Review of Literature*, while troubled by what a 'communist critic' might make of *The Waves*, considered the novel to be a 'multiple reflection of a dying race, this twilight of small souls' that lacks a 'more vital sense of life' (*CH* 280) and appeals only to 'the acclaim of a clique' (*CH* 281).

More recent critics have commented on the novel's eloquent silence, symbolic universality and sense of cosmic unity. Emotional, mystical readings tend to emphasise Bernard as spokesman for Woolf's own artistic vision, and to find harmony between characters. But others find the characters contestatory, and Bernard's role as ambivalent. Yet the lyricism of *The Waves* dominates critical responses. The novel is sometimes read as (auto)biographical. Mystical and aesthetic analogies are favoured by many critics, along with a dominant and lasting strand of Bergsonism. But more recent feminist and postcolonial readings have focused on its feminine textuality, and opened up its antipatriarchal, lesbian, suffragist, and anti-imperial subtexts.

Suggested further reading

Gillian Beer, *'The Waves*: "The Life of Anybody" ', in Beer, *Virginia Woolf: The Common Ground* (Edinburgh: Edinburgh University Press, 1996)

Jane Marcus, 'Britannia Rules the Waves', in Marcus, *Hearts of Darkness: White Women Write Race* (New Brunswick, NJ: Rutgers University Press, 2004)

Annette Oxindine, 'Sapphist Semiotics in Woolf's *The Waves*: Untelling and Retelling What Cannot be Told', in Vara Neverow-Turk and Mark Hussey (eds.), *Virginia Woolf: Themes and Variations* (New Brunswick, NJ, and London: Rutgers University Press, 2004)

Eric Warner, *Virginia Woolf: The Waves* (Cambridge: Cambridge University Press, 1987)

Flush: A Biography (1933)

Flush is a spoof biography. It is a comedic, fictional account of the life of Elizabeth Barrett Browning's spaniel, with ten illustrations, including four drawings by Vanessa Bell. It was for Woolf another spree, a relief between more serious projects. *Flush*'s very transgression and destabilisation of the categories of 'high' and 'low' art make it a satirical allegory of canon formation. Woolf herself seemed baffled by it during its composition, considering it 'too slight & too serious', and despaired of 'how to make anything of it' (*F* 134). It may certainly baffle the reader who comes to it after the poetic heights of *The Waves*. Further to its detriment, *Flush* rapidly became a huge bestseller, as a Book Society and Book-of-the-Month Club choice, and as such was considered a fall from high-brow grace by some contemporary reviewers and most subsequent Woolf critics. In recent years it has received more measured and interesting critical analysis, but it has yet to receive proper critical scrutiny.

Along with *Orlando* and *Roger Fry*, *Flush* is one of three of Woolf's works with the subtitle 'A Biography'. *Roger Fry* is the most straightforward of the three, being a more or less straight biography of Woolf's art critic friend. But like *Orlando*, *Flush* is an experimental biography. It is based on Woolf's knowledge of the real dog, Flush, gleaned from the letters of Robert Browning and Elizabeth Barrett Browning. She saw Rudolf Besier's successful play, *The Barretts of Wimpole Street*, in 1930, and this may have encouraged her interest in Flush's story. Woolf was also wanting 'to play a joke on Lytton [Strachey] – it was to parody him', but Strachey died in January 1932 before it was finished.

Flush is in six chapters, the first of which delineates Flush's genealogy and relates the circumstances of his birth. The opening line plays on Jane Austen's famous opening line to *Pride and Prejudice*: 'It is universally admitted that the family from which the subject of this memoir claims descent is one of the greatest antiquity' (*F* 7). By discussing the etymology of the name Spaniel, as well as the breeding history of these dogs, Woolf is able to satirise the aristocratic interest in human lineage:

> Some historians say that when the Carthaginians landed in Spain the common soldiers shouted with one accord 'Span! Span!' – for rabbits darted from every scrub, from every bush. The land was alive with rabbits. And Span in the Carthaginian tongue signifies Rabbit. Thus the land was called Hispania, or Rabbit-land, and the dogs, which were almost instantly perceived in full pursuit of the rabbits, were called Spaniels or rabbit dogs.   (*F* 7–8)

Given that Woolf's own spaniel, Pinka, posed for the frontispiece photograph of *Flush*, and was a gift from her lover, Vita Sackville-West, it is not difficult to read these opening salvos of *Flush* as a further reprise on Vita's own acclaimed Spanish ancestry, which Woolf had explored in *Orlando: A Biography*. The spaniel's aristocratic lineage is traced back to 'Wales in the middle of the tenth century', and it is explained that 'the spaniel was already a dog of value and reputation': 'He had his place already by the King's side. His family was held in honour before those of many famous monarchs. He was taking his ease in palaces when the Platagenets and the Tudors and the Stuarts were following other people's ploughs through other people's mud' (*F* 9).

The breeding points of the Spaniel Club are invoked to assess Flush's appearance, and comparison made with the 'Herald's College' in 'human society' (*F* 11). The genealogy of Flush's first owners, the Mitford family, is then discussed. Flush was born in 1842, and was given as a gift from the writer Mary Mitford to Elizabeth Barrett. Woolf describes Flush's olfactory and sensory experience of his first encounter with the Barrett household: 'only the sensations of . . . an explorer into the buried vaults of a ruined city can compare with the riot of emotions that flooded Flush's nerves as he stood for the first time in an invalid's bedroom, in Wimpole Street, and smelt eau-de-Cologne' (*F* 23). Her description of the Barrett household's interior is one of Woolf's nods to Strachey's debunking of Victoriana: 'Nothing in the room was itself; every thing was something else. Even the window blind was not a simple muslin blind; it was a painted fabric with a design of castles and gateways and groves of trees, and there were several peasants taking a walk' (*F* 24). When Flush gazes on his new mistress for the first time, it is as if he is looking in a mirror: 'Each was surprised. Heavy curls hung down on either side of Miss Barrett's face; large bright eyes shone out; a large mouth smiled. Heavy ears hung down on either side of Flush's face; his eyes, too, were large and bright: his mouth was wide. As they gazed at each other each felt: Here am I' (*F* 26). This momentary recognition between woman poet and her dog may correspond with Woolf's point in *A Room of One's Own* that 'Women have not had a dog's chance of writing poetry' (*AROO* 163).

In Chapter Two, 'The Back Bedroom', Flush is shown settling to his new urban life, 'led on chains' in Regent's Park, and closeted with Miss Barrett 'lying couched' (*F* 41) at her feet as she languishes, writes and receives visitors. Chapter Three, 'The Hooded Man', describes Robert Browning's courtship of his mistress from Flush's point of view. He jealously bites Browning, but is eventually forgiven by Elizabeth Barrett. At the close of the chapter, he is stolen. Chapter Four, 'Whitechapel', describes the Rookery slums where Flush is held for ransom, and the inequities of class are writ large: 'The racket, the hunger and the thirst, the reeking smells of the place – and once, Flush remembered, he had detested the scent of eau-de-Cologne – were fast obliterating any clear image, any single desire' (*F* 83). When Flush is returned to Elizabeth Barrett, she is about to elope with Robert Browning to Italy.

Flush's life there is the topic of Chapter Five, 'Italy'. One of the first things Flush notices about Italy is its more democratic society:

> in London he could scarcely trot round to the pillarbox without
> meeting some pug dog, retriever, bulldog, mastiff, collie,
> Newfoundland, St Bernard, fox terrier or one of the seven famous
> families of the Spaniel tribe. To each he gave a different name, and to
> each a different rank. But here in Pisa, though dogs abounded, there
> were no ranks; all – could it be possible? – were mongrels . . . Had the
> Kennel club, then, no jurisdiction in Italy?   (*F* 105)

When Flush returns to London for a visit, the unfortunate experiences of another dog owned by writers apparently confirms his preference for the democratic freedoms of Italy over the inequities of England. Nero, the pet dog of Thomas and Jane Carlyle, is described. His suicidal leap from a window is recounted, and his lingering death after the wheels of a butcher's cart crushed his throat. Returning to Italy, Flush is sea-sick at the mention of Mr Carlyle. Chapter Six, facetiously entitled 'The End', marks Flush's latter days and ends with a perfunctory account of his death: 'He had been alive; he was now dead. That was all.' (*F* 150). Yet Woolf's account of his Victorian life is also a dark critique of England and Italy in the 1930s under the shadow of fascism.

Although pleasantly reviewed by most of the press, including the *Times Literary Supplement*, the bestselling *Flush* was considered by the poet Geoffrey Grigson 'the most tiresome book which Mrs Woolf has yet written' (*D4* 184–5), and the *Granta* reviewer held that its 'deadly facility . . . combined with its popular success mean . . . the end of Mrs Woolf as a live force' (*D4* 186). And a sense of embarrassment coloured critical reception of *Flush* thereafter. For a while it was largely ignored in the burgeoning academic scholarship on Woolf. But more recently it has been read as political satire, as an allegory of Woolf's affair with Vita Sackville-West, and as a feminist narrative anticipating *The Years*. It is clearly ripe for more sustained critical attention.

Suggested further reading

Pamela Caughie, 'Flush and the Literary Canon: Oh Where Oh Where has that Little Dog Gone?', *Tulsa Studies in Women's Literature* 10 (1991), pp. 47–66

Craig Smith, 'Across the Widest Gulf: Nonhuman Subjectivity in Virginia Woolf's Flush', *Twentieth Century Literature* 48.3 (2002), pp. 348–61

Anna Snaith, 'Of Fanciers, Footnotes, and Fascism: Virginia Woolf's Flush', *Modern Fiction Studies* 48 (2002), pp. 614–36

Susan Squier, *Virginia Woolf and London: The Sexual Politics of the City* (Chapel Hill: University of North Carolina Press, 1985)

The Years (1937)

The Years is in the shape of a family 'saga' novel, and marks Woolf's return to a more conservative novelistic form. It is a chronological, and somewhat elegiac, account of the Pargiters, a middle-class family in London, from 1880 to 'the present day', presented in eleven chapters, each allocated, and entitled with, a sample, apparently arbitrary, year, and each opening with a descriptive passage on the elements and the seasons. Readers, nevertheless, sometimes find it difficult to get a purchase on this narrative since no one character is central. The lives of its various characters – Eleanor, Kitty, Rose, Martin, Sara, Peggy and North – are seen caught up in, and pitted against, the social, imperial and martial forces and institutions of patriarchal capitalism. Growing out of her drafting of the paper 'Professions for Women', a speech to the National Society for Womens' Service, Woolf's original project, *The Pargiters: A Novel-Essay*, was a very different and much more experimental piece, but, after lengthy compositional agonies, it diverged into two books, her feminist and pacifist tract, *Three Guineas* (1938), and 'that misery The Years' (*D5* 340). The novel is a radical feminist critique of its time, examining women's negotiation of domestic and public spheres. *The Years* also combines Woolf's interest in visionary and mythic matriarchal sources (notably in the work of the Cambridge classicist Jane Harrison) with her materialist-feminist social analysis. In retrospect, Woolf saw the novel as a failure. It certainly failed to meet some of her original ambitions for it, and she made the point 'that I myself know why its a failure, & that its failure is deliberate' (*D5* 65).

Woolf's ambition for the work that became *The Years* was that in it she 'must be bold & adventurous. I want to give the whole of the present society – nothing less: facts, as well as the vision. And to combine them both.' She saw the combining of fact and vision, granite and rainbow, in this new novel in terms of combining the styles of her two most different, previous novels: 'I mean, The Waves going on simultaneously with Night & Day. Is this possible?' (*D4* 151–2). The opening pastoral passage in each chapter of *The Years* does recall the poetic pastoral interludes of *The Waves*, and the depiction of the struggle of generations of women to negotiate the politics of private, family and public life does resemble *Night and Day*. Yet *The Years* itself is the result of a split in the previous draft work, *The Pargiters*, in which fact and vision combined in terms of nonfiction and fiction, propaganda and art. Woolf chose to split off the art into *The Years* and the propaganda into *Three Guineas*. In this sense she did fail to keep the two contained within one work. But this failure is to be understood in the context of her creative struggle to reconcile these two dynamics of compositional impetus; and to some extent those dynamics remain in *The Years*. Her main initial purpose, to write 'about the sexual life of women', still influences both works.

Woolf derived the name Pargiter, the surname of her fictional family, from the term 'parget', which means to whitewash, patch over, suppress, and it is found in the dialect dictionary of Joseph Wright, who appears in the Oxford section of *The Years* as Mr Robson. The word resonates in *The Years* in political and psychoanalytical terms. The Pargiters are seen at different historical moments attempting to smooth over political conflicts and crises as well as to suppress primal emotions. Similarly, Woolf herself has been considered a pargeter in her editing out of more incendiary passages in *The Years*. (The Oxford World's Classic edition of the novel gives two such excised sections in its Appendix.) But this honing of her text increases its surface tension so that 'each sentence though perfectly natural dialogue has a great pressure of meaning behind it' (*D4* 282). Given the final length of *The Years*, it may be argued that Woolf was not enough of a pargeter. However, the self-conscious pargeting of the novel itself also explains Woolf's sense of deliberate failure, since to expose the process of pargeting, pargeting itself must fail in its aim of completely smoothing over. For example, the pastoral passages that introduce each dated section are not typographically stylised as the italicised interludes are in *The Waves*, so that the transition to the social scene and dialogue is smoother in *The Years*, but the difference in textual surface is nevertheless noticeable.

In the first point of transition between opening pastoral and first historical section, the pastoral closes with a description of the moon rising: 'its polished coin, though obscured now and then by wisps of cloud, shone out with serenity, with severity, or perhaps with complete indifference. Slowly wheeling, like the rays of a searchlight, the days, the weeks, the years passed one after another across the sky' (*Y* 2). Here, the moon is figured as money, and the passage of time as a sinister factory or military light. The natural world and the passing of seasons are tainted by the metaphors of commerce and industrial warfare. This colours our reading of the opening line in the juxtaposed section on 1880, in which 'Colonel Abel Pargiter was sitting after luncheon in his club talking' (*Y* 2). In turn, we may reread the commercial discourse in the pastoral scene as itself coloured – indeed, pargeted – by the talk emanating from that bastion of imperial privilege, Colonel Pargiter's club. Indeed, in *Three Guineas*, the polemical essay that emanated from the draft that became *The Years*, Woolf describes the moon as a 'white sixpence' (*TG* 172). As these few lines of description demonstrate, the political satire in *The Years* includes a self-conscious metanarrative on how imperialist politics affects pastoral aesthetics, opening up the question of the relationship between the representation of the political and the politics of representation. The modernist sense of textual self-consciousness is central, then, to this apparently 'realist text'.

Woolf was attempting, in her self-conscious pargeting process, to

> keep one toe on the ground by means of dates, facts; envelop the whole in a changing temporal atmosphere; Compose into one vast many sided group at the end; and then shift the stress from present to future; and show the old fabric insensibly changing without death or violence into the future – suggesting there is no break, but a continuous development, possibly a recurrence of some pattern; of which of course we actors are ignorant. And the future was gradually to dawn. Of course I completely failed.   (*L6* 115–16)

Instead of representing change in terms of violent rupture and upheaval, then, she chooses to show the way such rupture occurs but is contained in the flux of social cohesion; hence her modernist eschewal of plot in *The Years*: 'Because I think action generally unreal. Its the thing we do in the dark that is more real' (*L6* 122). Whereas Woolf represented such change in *To the Lighthouse* through the compositional design of 'two blocks joined by a corridor', and in *The Waves* by rhythmic alternation between interludes and soliloquies, in *The Years* she projects it as 'a curiously uneven time sequence – a series of great balloons, linked by straight narrow passages of narrative' (*D4* 142).

The sequence of historical snapshots, or 'balloons', is certainly uneven, and apparently arbitrary. The first three chapters are quite evenly spaced in their temporal designation: the first is '1880'; the second is '1891'; the third is '1907'. Then comes a closer cluster of years: '1908'; '1910'; '1911'; '1913'; '1914'; '1917'; '1918'. Then there is a leap to 'The Present Day', which is set in the 1930s. The narrative restrains itself from full and direct representation of major action, and important events are filtered in as received, or inferred, information, impinging on domestic and everyday scenes. The opening chapter describes the Pargiter family in 1880, as the father returns from his club and from visiting his mistress to a household that awaits the imminent death of his ailing wife, Rose. We are introduced to his elder daughters Delia, Milly and Eleanor Pargiter and to the youngsters, Martin and Rose. The daughters are subordinated around the tea-table and burdened by other domestic duties. There are two other brothers, Morris, who is a legal clerk, and Edward, who is a student at Oxford. Rose goes out illicitly and is frightened by a man exposing himself in the street, an experience that marks her for life. Meanwhile Eleanor, sitting by her mother's sickbed, dreams of the Irish leader Charles Stewart Parnell. Edward is described in Oxford reading *Antigone*, and a glimpse of his undergraduate friendships is given. His cousin Kitty is described thinking of him and rejecting him in her mind as a marriage prospect; her mother is described receiving news of his mother's (her cousin's) death.

Eleven years later, in '1891', Kitty is now Lady Lasswade, having married the titled suitor approved by her mother. Edward is a don. Morris and Milly have married. Eleanor is involved in a project to house the poor. She receives a letter from Martin relating his adventures in the jungle while serving in India. As the death of Parnell, a man brought down by an affair, is reported, we meet Colonel Pargiter troubled by this as he visits his brother Sir Digby Pargiter and family. The focus shifts in '1907' and '1908' to Martin, who has returned from India, Sir Digby's wife Eugenie and daughters Maggie and Sara, and Rose who has become a political activist for the cause of feminism. In '1910', the year in which Woolf famously remarked that 'human character changed' (in the essay 'Mr Bennett and Mrs Brown') Rose is attending suffragette meetings, Maggie and Sara share an apartment, and Kitty Lasswade attends the opera. The death of Edward VII is announced. In '1911' Rose has been arrested for throwing a brick (suffragette activism).

Eleanor visits her brother Morris's family, including her niece and nephew Peggy and North. She reads Dante. It is inferred that Colonel Pargiter has died. In '1913', with the house sold, Eleanor releases their servant Crosby who goes into lodgings and still takes care of Martin's laundry. Martin reflects on his father's secret affair, discovered after his death.

A dinner party thrown by Kitty Lasswade features in the lengthy section '1914', at which Martin feels excluded. Earlier he lunches with Sara and they meet Maggie in Hyde Park; they walk by Speakers' Corner, reflecting on relationships. Rose has been jailed. In '1917' North Pargiter is reported to be on his way to the front while Eleanor dines with Maggie and her husband in a basement during an air raid; another guest, Nicholas, is revealed to be homosexual; Eleanor returns home by bus. In the brief '1918' section, Crosby is cursing her lot, and the war is over. The 'Present Day' section culminates in a party thrown by Delia and attended by all the surviving Pargiters. Before this Peggy, now a doctor, and North, who has returned from farming in Africa, visit their aunt Eleanor. North dines with Sara in her modest lodgings while Peggy and Eleanor make their way to Delia's party. Arbitrary and elliptical signs of the threatening international political scene occur, such as Eleanor's ripping of a newspaper. Sara tells North of the Jew who persists in leaving the bathtub dirty. (Does Woolf here expose and criticise anti-Semitism or merely reinscribe it? Critics are divided on this point.) At the party there is an air of social tension and unease. North chances on a volume of Catullus's poetry, and reflects on the naïve political acumen of the younger people there. Nicholas and Sara converse warmly. As dawn breaks, the children of the caretaker sing an unintelligible song, and as people leave Eleanor watches a couple getting out of a taxi further down the street, a sight that recalls a key image in *A Room of One's Own*. A forlorn, elegiac tone presides.

Woolf was worried that she would be 'laughed at' and 'held up to scorn and ridicule' (*D5* 64) on publication of *The Years*. Leonard Woolf kept from her his thoughts that it was, with *Night and Day*, her worst work. Yet John Maynard Keynes thought it her best (*D5* 77). The *Times Literary Supplement* reviewer found it a 'penetrating but uneventful chronicle' that 'needs more than one reading', and addresses 'change and continuity', showing that 'the illuminating moments of life are discontinuous'. It also considered that all the 'important characters are women' (*CH* 369). Edwin Muir's review was mixed, recognising that Woolf 'is incomparable when she is evoking a sense of simultaneity in time. But the pattern she stretches over the story strikes one as cold and artificial' (*CH* 389). He thought that as a chronicle it had 'a perfect beginning and a perfect end, and almost no middle' (*CH* 390). But he defined Woolf's art as giving 'a quality of pleasure in living, a lovely sense of people thinking and feeling and brooding by themselves, with vague memories and sharp present sensations, with bits of song and odd poetry; and still their contact with life, in 1880 or 1920, is quite definitely realised' (*CH* 391). More recent critics have recognised and examined the novel's intense interest in women's experiences, and the rhythms and expectations of courtship and sexuality, within the frame of industrial capitalism and imperialism – the interplay of private and public spheres.

Suggested further reading

Patricia Cramer, '*Vita Nuova*: Courtly Love and Lesbian Romance in *The Years*', *Woolf Studies Annual* 10 (2004), pp. 173–202

Mitchell A. Leaska, 'Virginia Woolf, the Pargeter: A Reading of *The Years*', *Bulletin of the New York Public Library* 80.2 (1977), pp. 172–210

Grace Radin, *Virginia Woolf's The Years: The Evolution of a Novel* (Knoxville: Tennessee University Press, 1981)

Susan Squier, 'The Politics of City Space in *The Years*: Street Love, Pillar Boxes and Bridges', in Jane Marcus (ed.), *New Feminist Essays on Virginia Woolf* (Lincoln and London: University of Nebraska Press, 1981)

Between the Acts (1941)

Between the Acts, Woolf's last novel, was published shortly after her death. Woolf had not finalised the manuscript and certain features were decided upon, after her death, by Leonard Woolf. The novel returns to a more stylised and streamlined form, and seems to achieve Woolf's ambition to produce a lyric novel-drama. It is fluid in form, chapterless and sectionless. Woolf's technique collapses history, politics and feminism into densely allusive, highly charged imagistic prose, to which all semblance of plot is sacrificed.

Between the Acts comprises a sequence of scenes from an English village on a summer's evening in the Oliver family house, Pointz Hall, and the following day, on which the annual pageant takes place. Many of the villagers participate in this satirical romp, in various kinds of theatrical tableaux, through the history of England, under the direction of the eccentric Miss La Trobe. The novel bristles with the menace of incipient fascism and impending war. The main characters are depicted in action and dialogue, interwoven with the italicised passages of the pageant's performance, itself punctuated by various incidental natural and manmade events, such as a sudden downpouring of rain, the flitting of birds, and the flight of military aeroplanes, all of which complicate the boundaries between art and life. In the interstices the marital tensions between Isa and Giles Oliver are explored, as well as the larger pulses and oppositional tensions of wider, collective life.

Woolf began thinking about writing this novel in August 1937 when she asked herself 'Will another novel ever swim up?' and got the 'hint that it's to be dialogue: and poetry: and prose; all quite distinct' (*D5* 105). In April she finds herself 'sketching out a new book', but she wanted something less burdensome than *The Years* had been to write, and something to alleviate her from the tedium of writing her friend Roger Fry's biography: 'only don't please impose that huge burden on me again, I implore. Let it be random & tentative; something I can blow of a morning, to relieve myself of Roger: don't, I implore, lay down a scheme; call in all the cosmic immensities; & force my tired & diffident brain to embrace another whole – all parts contributing – not yet awhile' (*D5* 135).

Woolf's early conception of the provisionally titled 'Pointz Hall' was that it was to be light in touch after the serious, visionary work of the troublesome *The Years* (perhaps like *Orlando*, coming after *To the Lighthouse*): 'But to amuse myself, let me note: why not Poyntzet Hall: a centre: all lit. discussed in connection with real little incongruous living humour; & anything that comes into my head; but "I" rejected: "We" substituted: to whom at the end there shall be an invocation?' Yet the new project seems to resemble *The Years* in this concern with collective rather than individual experience. Woolf continues: ' "We" . . . composed of many different things . . . we all life, all art, all waifs & strays – rambling capricious but somehow unified whole – the present state of my mind?' (*D5* 135). However, in encountering the final form, the reader does not experience the lack of purchase on the circle of characters that seems to be the case with *The Years*. Instead of accounting for the passage of years, *Between the Acts*, like *Mrs Dalloway*, is set during one day. It resembles *To the Lighthouse* and *Orlando* (and parts of *The Voyage Out* and *The Waves*) in its country house setting: 'And English country; & a scenic old house – & a terrace where nursemaids walk? & people passing – & perpetual variety & change from intensity to prose. & facts. – & notes; & – but eno' (*D5* 135). Once again, Woolf invokes the contrary dynamics of prose and poetry, fact and vision, granite and rainbow.

It is important to remember that the factual elements informing Woolf's composition became more sinister as time passed. By the time she was in the process of writing this novel, she was living in a country at war with Nazi Germany. Much of *Between the Acts* was written in 1940, during a period of dark, momentous historical events such as Dunkirk, the Battle of Britain, the London Blitz and the fall of France. And the novel is set in June, 1939, on the brink of war. The title itself seems to reflect this dark threshold, narrowly between the Spanish Civil War (in which Woolf lost her nephew) and the Second World War, and more broadly between the Great War and the Second World War. Again the larger historical events elliptically inform the private sphere of the novel, and its ostensible public domain is no larger than a small English village. The historical, political and factual elements are nevertheless balanced by the mythic, poetic and aesthetic in this novel. As in *To the Lighthouse*, a work of art is central to *Between the Acts*. This time it is a village pageant rather than a painting, but it serves similarly as a self-reflexive analogue for the novel in which it appears. Miss La Trobe is an artist figure, just like Lily Briscoe. In this respect *Between the Acts* is a Künstlerroman.

Isa Oliver is herself a secret poet. And like the pageant, her compositions are interrupted by the intrusions of other people and the external realm around her. Early in the novel she sits at her dressing table reflecting on the desire aroused in her by Rupert Haines, the local married gentleman-farmer, and this reflection transmutes into poetic composition as she remembers the effect of his words which could 'lie between them like a wire, tingling, tangling, vibrating – she groped, in the depths of the looking-glass for a word to fit the infinitely quick vibrations of the aeroplane propeller that she had seen once at dawn at Croydon' (*BA* 20–1). Isa seems to have found in this piece of modern technology the 'objective correlative' for her emotion, as Woolf's friend T. S. Eliot's theory might have it. The telephone interrupts her train of compositional thought, and she finds herself in dialogue about the fish order: '"There to lose what binds us here," she murmured. "Soles. Filleted. In time for lunch please," she said aloud. "With a feather, a blue feather . . . flying mounting through the air . . . there to lose what binds us here . . ." The words weren't worth writing in the book bound like an account book in case Giles suspected. "Abortive" was the word that expressed her' (*BA* 21). This scene represents an avant-garde aesthetic process that is collage-like in its juxtaposing of different discourses, and extends beyond the individual lyric impulse to include other voices and incidental objects.

Isa's stockbroker husband, Giles, meanwhile is attracted to the colourful Mrs Manresa, who arrives for lunch with William Dodge, a homosexual, who is himself attracted to Giles, but is also emotionally close to Isa. In one of the most disturbing scenes in the novel, Giles is depicted, during the interval of the pageant, kicking stones, an action that he correlates with his turbulent emotions: 'The first kick was Manresa (lust). The second, Dodge (perversion). The third himself (coward). And the fourth and the fifth and all the others were the same' (*BA* 118). His violence then transfers to living creatures when he comes across the grotesque spectacle of a snake in the grass, 'choked with a toad in its mouth. The snake was unable to swallow; the toad was unable to die . . . a monstrous inversion. So, raising his foot, he stamped on them' (*BA* 119). This single act of violence seems to represent the raising of the fascist jackboot in the wider international sphere of impending war: 'Action relieved him. He strode to the Barn, with blood on his shoes' (*BA* 119).

The pageant formally closes with an avant-garde gesture, when the actors assemble on stage turning mirrors of all sizes on the audience, and a voice 'from the bushes – megaphontic, anonymous, loud-speaking affirmation' addresses them: '*All you can see of yourselves is scraps, orts and fragments? Well then listen to the gramophone affirming . . .*' (*BA* 218, 220). In the aftermath the misunderstood lesbian outsider, Miss La Trobe, who fits in neither with the assembled aristocracy in the audience nor with the villagers she has organised in her performance, is seen glimpsing the beginnings of her next work. Hearing the gossip about her in the pub cease as she enters:

> She took her chair and looked through the smoke at a crude glass painting of a cow in a stable; also a cock and a hen. She raised her glass to her lips. And drank. And listened. Words of one syllable sank down into the mud. She drowsed; she nodded. The mud became fertile. Words rose above the intolerably laden dumb oxen plodding through the mud. Words without meaning – wonderful words.   (*BA* 247–8)

This mythic, chthonic language issues from the mud, much like the song of the flowerseller in *Mrs Dalloway*. These primal syllables resemble both ancient utterances and contemporary avant-garde poetics. But the novel closes with the ambivalent passions of Giles and Isa in confrontation, encapsulated by two brief but powerful sentences: 'Then the curtain rose. They spoke' (*BA* 256). The opening of dialogue at this moment in the text allows us not only to reflect on the particularly poignant and exposed, dark historical moment of the novel's writing and first publication, but also to reflect on the dialogues this text initiates with our own times. What are Giles and Isa saying outside the confines of *Between the Acts*?

Edwin Muir, reviewing *Between the Acts*, called it one of Woolf's 'most perfect novels': 'She has never written better prose than the prose in this last book, with its flashing, almost imperious curtness, its exact colouring, and its rapid, unhesitating movement' (*CH* 443). Yet Frank Swinerton, in his review for the *Observer*, encapsulated an enduring myth about Woolf's supposed otherworldliness by suggesting that 'she had almost no practical experience of life. She was like somebody bedridden in a house in the country . . . occasionally quite piercingly uncovering a mood or attitude, but incapable of more than subtle guesswork about her own species.' He concludes, astonishingly, that she, 'with all her gifts, could never test intuition by any but literary and conversational contacts with reality' (*CH* 442). Malcolm Cowley, for the *New Republic*, at least recognised that Woolf's last novel 'is her comment on the war, or rather her elegy for the society the war was destroying', before warming to the myth that she was not equipped to inhabit the real world: 'When the bombs crashed through the glass that covered England, she was one of the people – and they were not the weaklings or the cowards – who were too finely organized for life in the wind and the rain' (*CH* 449).

As such reviews suggest, critical responses to *Between the Acts* were at first coloured by the aftermath of Woolf's suicide at a low point in the war: and it has been called 'the longest suicide note in the English language'. The book's relation to her suicide and to the wider context of war continue to exercise critics, but there is a wealth of other material exploring everything from sexual politics to avant-garde technique, and how such things might be related. Woolf's polyphonic technique has been seen as both unifying and endlessly transgressive and open. The mythic and prehistoric subtexts of *Between the Acts* have yielded psychoanalytical, political and feminist readings.

Suggested further reading

Gillian Beer, 'The Island and the Aeroplane: the Case of Virginia Woolf', in Beer, *Virginia Woolf: The Common Ground* (Edinburgh: Edinburgh University Press, 1996)

Stuart Christie, 'Willing Epigone: Virginia Woolf's *Between the Acts* as Nietzschean Historiography', *Woolf Studies Annual* 8 (2002), pp. 157–74

Mark Hussey, ' "I" Rejected; "We" Substituted: Self and Society in *Between the Acts*', in Bege K. Bowers and Barbara Brothers (eds.), *Reading and Writing Women's Lives: A Study of the Novel of Manners* (Ann Arbor, MI: UMI Research Press, 1990)

Frank Kermode, 'Introduction', in Virginia Woolf, *Between the Acts*, ed. Kermode (Oxford: Oxford University Press, 1992)

Patricia Laurence, 'The Facts and Fugue of War: From *Three Guineas* to *Between the Acts*', in Mark Hussey (ed.), *Virginia Woolf and War: Fiction, Reality, and Myth* (New York: Pace University Press, 1992)

Short stories

Virginia Woolf wrote a number of short stories, many of which were published in her lifetime. These have long been acknowledged as significant contributions to the genre, and some mark important points of departure in the genesis of Woolf's experimental fictional style. The short story is a prominent feature in modernism since the form lends itself to expression of the momentary and fragmentary nature of experience that preoccupies many modernist writers. Woolf is the author of several stories that have become frequently anthologised landmarks of modernist literature, and her stories are also prominent in several feminist anthologies. The stories as a whole range from the highly experimental and abstract to the fairly traditional in form, and they are also marked by elegant economy, poignancy and wit. They span her writing career: she wrote her first story, 'Phyllis and Rosamund', in 1906, and her last, 'The Watering Place', in 1941. The very first publication of the Hogarth Press was *Two Stories* (1917), comprising Leonard Woolf's 'Three Jews' and Virginia Woolf's 'The Mark on the Wall'. She published one other collection in her lifetime, *Monday or Tuesday* (1921), which included eight stories: 'The Mark on the Wall', 'Kew Gardens', 'An Unwritten Novel', 'A Haunted House', 'A Society', 'Monday or Tuesday', 'The String Quartet' and 'Blue & Green'. A limited edition of *Kew Gardens* appeared in 1919.

A further nine stories were published in various journals and magazines during Woolf's lifetime: 'Solid Objects' (1920), 'Mrs Dalloway in Bond Street' (1923), 'A Woman's College from Outside' (1926), 'The New Dress' (1927), 'Moments of Being: Slater's Pins Have No Points' (1928), 'The Lady in the Looking-Glass: A Reflection' (1930), 'The Shooting Party' (1938), 'The Duchess and the Jeweller' (1938), and 'Lappin and Lapinova' (1938). After the completion of her novel *Mrs Dalloway* in 1925, Woolf wrote eight stories concerning guests at Mrs Dalloway's party, only the first of which was published in her lifetime: 'The New Dress', 'Happiness', 'Ancestors', 'The Introduction', 'Together and Apart', 'The Man Who Loved His Kind', 'A Simple Melody' and 'A Summing Up'. These have been collected, with 'Mrs Dalloway in Bond Street' and the novel itself, in *The Mrs Dalloway Reader* (2005). There are around twenty other stories, which were published posthumously. All are collected in Susan Dick's edition, *The Complete Shorter Fiction of Virginia Woolf* (1989). A selection are discussed below.

Woolf understood **'The Mark on the Wall'** (1917), one of her most famous short stories, as a key point of transition in her compositional methodology. This story, with 'Kew Gardens' and 'An Unwritten Novel', she came to think of as 'dancing in unity' (*D2* 14) with her early conception of her first experimental novel, *Jacob's Room* (1922), which itself was to have 'no sca-ffolding' (*D2* 13). 'The Mark on the Wall' is indeed in the form of an unstructured reverie prompted by the narrator's catching sight of a mark on the wall of a domestic interior: 'How readily our thoughts swarm upon a new object' (*CSF* 83). The narrator at first thinks that it may have been made by a nail, and from this considers what pictures the previous occupants of the house might have hung there. This leads to thoughts on the transience of life, which is likened to being blown through the Tube at fifty miles an hour – landing at the other end without a single hairpin in one's hair! Shot out at the feet of God entirely naked! Tumbling head over heels in the asphodel meadows like brown paper parcels pitched down a shoot in the post office! With one's hair flying back like the tail of a racehorse. Yes, that seems to express the rapidity of life, the perpetual waste and repair; all so casual, all so haphazard . . . (*CSF* 84)

Woolf figures life as high-speed mechanised industrial process, and then turns to consider 'afterlife' in which humans are indistinguishable from vegetation: 'as for saying which are trees, and which are men and women, or whether there are such things, that one won't be in a condition to do for fifty years or so. There will be nothing but spaces of light and dark, intersected by thick stalks, and rather higher up perhaps, rose-shaped blots of an indistinct colour' (*CSF* 84). The narrator jolts away from this sumptuous visual imagery to reconsider the mark on the wall as a blemish, and slides into another reverie, this time self-consciously seeking 'a track indirectly reflecting credit on myself' (*CSF* 85). The narrator considers how such flights construct a sense of the self: 'All the time I am dressing up the figure of myself in my own mind' (*CSF* 85). It is this very process that will become the stuff of novels 'in future' when novelists 'will realise more and more the importance of these reflections . . . those are the depths they will explore, those the phantoms they will pursue, leaving the description of reality more and more out of their stories, taking a knowledge of it for granted, as the Greeks did and Shakespeare perhaps' (*CSF* 85–6). This statement on the proper stuff of fiction comes close to Woolf's thoughts in her essay 'Modern Fiction' (see below) written around the same time. Having explored the interior consciousness of the self, the narrator then takes comfort in returning to contemplate the material, object world: 'Thus, waking from a midnight dream of horror, one hastily turns on the light and lies quiescent, worshipping the chest of drawers, worshipping solidity, worshipping reality, worshipping the impersonal world which is proof of some existence other than ours' (*CSF* 88).

At the close of the story, this emphasis on the object world culminates in 'a vast upheaval of matter', which is another person, who announces the intention to go and buy a newspaper. This ushers in other references to 'reality': 'Though it's no good buying newspapers . . . Nothing ever happens. Curse this war; God damn this war! . . . All the same, I don't see why we should have a snail on our wall' (*CSF* 89). Putting into practice the novelistic method of the future predicted earlier, the narrator delivers at the close of the story the marginal reality of newspapers and war, at the same time as the identity of the mark is revealed: 'Ah, the mark on the wall! It was a snail' (*CSF* 89). The reveries on what the mark might represent, from nail to snail, suggest a narrative self-consciousness that extends to question how we should read any representational language – whether in fiction or the newspaper. The very pressing matter of the war, and how it is to be represented, looms significantly at the story's margins.

The most famous of Woolf's short stories is probably **'Kew Gardens'** (1919). It has another snail as its point of focus. This time it is in the foliage of a flowerbed in the Royal Botanical Gardens at Kew. This pastoral narrative alternates between close-up description of the snail's activity and recorded snatches of various human conversations going on around the vicinity of the flowerbed. Woolf published two different editions of this story with woodcuts by Vanessa Bell (1919 and 1927), and these images interpenetrate with the verbal text. The juxtaposition of snaillife with humanlife is both comical and compelling.

Exchanges between four pairs of people are described as they are passing the flowerbed. The first is between the married couple Eleanor and Simon, who are followed by their children Caroline and Hubert. Simon remembers coming to this place fifteen years earlier and proposing to Lily. He remembers how the garden seemed to supply objective correlatives to his hopes and desires:

> 'my love and desire were in the dragon-fly; for some reason I thought that if it settled there, on that leaf, the broad one with the red flower in the middle of it, if the dragon-fly settled on the leaf she would say "Yes" at once. But the dragon-fly went round and round: it never settled anywhere – of course not, happily not, or I shouldn't be walking here with Eleanor and the children – Tell me Eleanor, d'you ever think of the past?' (*CSF* 91)

Eleanor affirms the garden's facility to conjure up the past. She recalls twenty years before being one of '"six little girls . . . down by a lake, painting the water-lilies, the first red water-lilies I'd ever seen. And suddenly a kiss, there on the back of my neck"' (*CSF* 91). This 'precious' experience, to which she has returned all her life, was 'the kiss of an old grey-haired woman with a wart on her nose, the mother of all my kisses all my life' (*CSF* 91). Whereas her husband recalls the unrequited love of past romantic courtship, Eleanor recalls a primal, maternal kiss, the memory of which prompts her to call her children: 'Come Caroline, come Hubert' (*CSF* 91). There is nevertheless an erotic charge to the memory of this kiss.

Focus now switches to the pastoral microcosm of the flowerbed where the snail is described 'labour[ing] over the crumbs of loose earth' (*CSF* 91). Simon's anecdote about his correlation of his proposal with the movements of a dragonfly suggest a narrative self-consciousness that encourages the reader to focus on the detailed description of snaillife as both a juxtaposed vignette of the real world and as a vehicle for further imposed meanings. Woolf's narrative is concerned with constructing and exposing such processes, showing how human thought and communication interpenetrates with the object world.

The second human pair to pass the flowerbed is that of two men, a younger man calmly accompanying an older and quite disturbed man, who babbles about the dead of the Great War, and who 'could be heard murmuring about forests of Uruguay blanketed with the wax petals of tropical roses, nightingales, sea beaches, mermaids and women drowned at sea, as he suffered himself to be moved on by William, upon whose face the look of stoical patience grew slowly deeper and deeper' (*CSF* 93). The inclusion of the mentally disturbed in the same pastoral continuum raises important and interesting questions about social and political inclusion, and about the impact of war on such peaceful, domestic scenes.

The next couple are 'two elderly women of the lower middle class, one stout and ponderous, the other rosy-cheeked and nimble' (*CSF* 93). A snatch of their 'very complicated dialogue' is given: '"Nell, Bert, Lot, Cess, Phil, Pa, he says, I says, she says, I says, I says" . . . "My Bert, Sis, Bill, Grandad . . . Sugar, flour, kippers, greens/Sugar, sugar sugar"' (*CSF* 93). The words shoot out in a surrealist stream, and the narrative becomes self-conscious, describing the mingling of words with the object world: 'The ponderous woman looked through the pattern of falling words at the flowers standing cool, firm and upright in the earth, with a curious expression' (*CSF* 93). Words take on material, if transparent, qualities as the woman lets 'the words fall over her' as if they are rain. Attention returns to the snail, which has 'now considered every possible method of reaching his goal without going round the dead leaf or climbing over it' (*CSF* 93).

A young man and woman, the fourth couple, come into view, and they seem to take on some of the characteristics of the flowerbed: 'They were both in the prime of youth, or even in the season which precedes the prime of youth, the season before the smooth pink folds of the flower have burst their gummy case, when the wings of the butterfly, though fully grown, are motionless in the sun' (*CSF* 94). The transition in metaphorical language moves surreally from vegetation to insect to human, as the couple flirtatiously discuss the prospect of tea. The narrative self-consciously explains how 'one couple after another with much the same irregular and aimless movement passed the flower-bed and were enveloped in layer after layer of green-blue vapour, in which at first their bodies had substance and a dash of colour, but later both substance and colour dissolved in the green-blue atmosphere' (*CSF* 95).

This stylised, painterly language celebrates artifice and the paradox of pattern in random movements. Voices are described as 'breaking the silence' but then the silence itself is brought into question: 'But there was no silence; all the time the motor omnibuses were turning their wheels and changing their gear; like a vast nest of Chinese boxes all of wrought steel turning ceaselessly one within another the city murmured; on the top of which the voices cried aloud and the petals of myriads of flowers flashed their colours into the air' (*CSF* 95). *Kew Gardens* celebrates the micro- and macrocosms of a city life that includes pastoral and urban mechanised experiences, inter-penetrating with human affairs, which are themselves communicated in terms of the intimate, individual and personal as well as the wider social and political scenes.

'Solid Objects' (1920) again runs the gamut of human experience, giving the extremes of a spectrum in one man's life: his growing and prized collection of discarded, broken objects gleaned from the beach and from urban wasteland, on the one hand, and on the other, his waning participation in the formal politics of parliament. The story begins by showing the human in minute dimensions against the close-up scale of a beach where the focus is first on John's tunnelling fingers as they uncover a 'lump of glass' in the sand (*CSF* 102), and then on the distant vista: 'The only thing that moved upon the vast semicircle of the beach was one small black spot' (*CSF* 102). This spot gradually comes into focus: 'it became apparent from a certain tenuity in its blackness that this spot possessed four legs; and moment by moment it became more unmistakable that it was composed of the persons of two young men' (*CSF* 102). They are arguing about politics. The narrative emphasizes their bodily materiality: 'nothing was so solid, so living, so hard, red, hirsute and virile as these two bodies for miles and miles of sea and sandhill' (*CSF* 102). While Charles skims stones on the sea, John finds a worn piece of glass: 'still working his fingers in the water, they curled round something hard – a full drop of solid matter – and gradually dislodged a large irregular lump, and brought it to the surface' (*CSF* 103). Whereas his friend happily casts away the stones he gleans, John keeps the glass for his mantelpiece, the first object in his prized collection. It serves as an interpenetrating object with his thought processes: 'Looked at again and again half consciously by a mind thinking of something else, any object mixes itself so profoundly with the stuff of thought that it loses its actual form and recomposes itself a little differently in an ideal shape which haunts the brain when we least expect it' (*CSF* 104). As John's collection of found objects increases, so his interest in political affairs and other people diminishes. By the close of the story, Charles, his political sparring partner, abandons him to his all-consuming passion for stones.

'**Blue & Green**' (1921) is a brief, abstract narrative in two paragraphs, and the most experimental and painterly of Woolf's stories. It seems to narrate itself from within a work of art. The first paragraph is entitled 'GREEN' and describes an arrangement of green objects: 'The pointed fingers of glass hang downwards. The light slides down the glass, and drops a pool of green. All day long the ten fingers of the lustre drop green upon the marble.' There is a surreal moment of synaesthesia when not just the 'feathers' but also the 'harsh cries' of 'parakeets' appear as 'sharp blades of palm trees – green, too; green needles glittering in the sun.' Sound is given coloured, material qualities. There is a downward slant to the composition, and it closes with the arrival of night when 'the needles drip blots of blue. The green's out' (*CSF* 142).

The second paragraph, entitled 'BLUE', describes an upward composition in blue, rising to meet the green: 'The snub-nosed monster rises to the surface and spouts through his blunt nostrils two columns of water, which, fiery-white in the centre, spray off into a fringe of blue beads. Strokes of blue line the black tarpaulin of his hide.' The monster appears to be a beached fish: 'Thrown upon the beach he lies, blunt, obtuse, shedding dry blue scales' (*CSF* 142). Another synaesthetic moment follows when a 'wave rolls beneath the blue bells', and 'bells' appears to refer to the sound emanating from the cathedral in the next, closing sentence: 'But the cathedral's different, cold, incense laden, faint blue with the veils of madonnas' (*CSF* 142). This scintillating arrangement approximates the status of a semi-abstract, verbal still-life. It is an exquisite object in itself. This is the most extreme and most compressed of Woolf's experimental works.

'**Moments of Being: Slater's Pins Have No Points**' (1928) is a classic modernist short story in its self-conscious rendering and exploration of a single, lyric moment. It describes a moment of intimacy between teacher and pupil: ' "Slater's pins have no points – don't you always find that?" said Miss Craye, turning round as the rose fell out of Fanny Wilmot's dress, and Fanny stooped with her ears full of the music, to look for the pin on the floor' (*CSF* 215). These words shock Fanny because they force her to think of her music teacher, who leads a precious, aesthetic, and privileged existence, as occupying the same mundane, material world as everyone else:

Did she stand at the counter waiting like anybody else, and was she given a bill with coppers wrapped in it, and did she slip them into her purse and then, an hour later, stand by her dressing table and take out the pins? . . . What need had she of pins – Julia Craye – who lived, it seemed, in the cool, glassy world of Bach fugues, playing to herself what she liked and only consenting to take one or two pupils at the Archer Street College of Music.   (*CSF* 215)

Fanny reads the question as a 'venture' by Miss Craye to connect on common ground. She also reflects on Miss Craye's enigmatic assertion that 'protection' was 'the only use of men' (*CSF* 217), and there is further speculation on the unmarried life of Miss Craye. At the close of the story, as Fanny finds the fallen pin, she surprises Miss Craye holding the flower (the 'rose' is now a 'carnation') 'in a moment of ecstasy', and they kiss: 'She saw Julia open her arms; saw her blaze; saw her kindle. Out of the night she burnt like a dead white star. Julia kissed her. Julia possessed her.' Miss Craye repeats her bridging statement: '"Slater's pins have no points"' (*CSF* 220). The celebratory inscription of this erotic moment between women was avant-garde for the time of its publication in 1928, given that Radclyffe Hall's lesbian novel, *The Well of Loneliness*, was banned for obscenity in the same year.

'The Lady in the Looking-Glass: A Reflection' (1930) is a sophisticated sketch of a domestic interior, which the narrator describes in great detail. The narrator likens herself to 'one of those naturalists who, covered with grass and leaves, lie watching the shyest animals – badgers, otters, kingfishers – moving about freely, themselves unseen. The room that afternoon was full of such shy creatures, lights and shadows, curtains blowing, petals falling — things that never happen, so it seems, if someone is looking' (*CSF* 221). It is the scene reflected in the hall mirror that especially occupies her attention: 'But, outside, the looking-glass reflected the hall table, the sunflowers, the garden path so accurately and so fixedly that they seemed held there in their reality unescapably [*sic*]. It was a strange contrast – all changing here, all stillness there. One could not help looking from one to the other' (*CSF* 221). The narrator describes an alarming moment of estrangement when '[a] large black form loomed into the looking-glass; blotted out everything, strewed the table with a packet of marble tablets veined with pink and grey, and was gone.' At first she can make no sense of this but 'then by degrees some logical process set to work on them and began ordering and arranging them and bringing them into the fold of common experience. One realised at last that they were merely letters. The man had brought the post' (*CSF* 223). She reflects on how the lady of the house, Isabella, will read the letters and hide them away. The looking-glass is a self-conscious framing device in the story.

In framing the delivery of unopened letters it seems to point up the futility of verbal language in the face of its own visual language. There are further speculations on the enigmatic Isabella, and at the close the narrator observes that to 'talk of "prizing her open" as if she were an oyster, to use any but the finest and subtlest and most pliable tools upon her was impious and absurd'. She then begins an attempt with the words 'One must imagine', but this train of thought is broken off: '– here was she in the looking-glass. It made one start' (*CSF* 225).

At first it is not clear whether Isabella is actually in the looking-glass or only imagined there, but the glass seems to exert a more and more exacting hold on her, and Isabella is observed in a cruel and cold light: 'Everything dropped from her – clouds, dress, basket, diamond – all that one had called the creeper and convolvulus. Here was the hard wall beneath. Here was the woman herself. She stood naked in that pitiless light.' This 'enthralling spectacle' reveals that 'there was nothing. Isabella was perfectly empty. She had no thoughts. She had no friends. She cared for nobody. As for her letters, they were all bills. Look, as she stood there, old and angular, veined and lined, with her high nose and her wrinkled neck, she did not even trouble to open them' (*CSF* 225). This chilling moment of revelation is humorously undercut by the tart last line of the story: 'People should not leave looking-glasses hanging in their rooms' (*CSF* 225).

'Lappin and Lapinova' (1938) is representative of Woolf's more discursive style and is one of her finest and funniest short stories. It proffers a scorching satirical analysis of marriage. Rosalind and Ernest keep their marriage alive by indulging in a joint fantasy world in which she is Queen Lapinova and he is King Lappin: 'Ernest had no objection to being that kind of rabbit, and since it amused her to see him twitch his nose – he had never known that his nose twitched – he twitched it on purpose' (*CSF* 261). At first this common fantasy and rabbit-language sustain their marriage, and Woolf's account of a dinner with Ernest's extended family is a tour-de-force, showing how their secret rabbit language buoys up the wife; but the husband is seen to grow more and more reluctant to take on the mantle of King Lapin, or to enter into their shared narratives. Eventually he returns home to find his wife distraught at losing her rabbit persona:

> 'Yes,' he said at length. 'Poor Lapinova . . .' He straightened his tie at the looking-glass over the mantelpiece.
>
> 'Caught in a trap,' he said, 'killed', and sat down and read the newspaper. (*CSF* 268)

The husband kills off the rabbits and all semblance of a shared language of love. The last line of the story devastatingly records the obvious: 'So that was the end of that marriage' (*CSF* 268).

Suggested further reading

Kathryn N. Benzel and Ruth Hoberman (eds.), *Trespassing Boundaries: Virginia Woolf's Short Fiction* (Basingstoke: Palgrave, 2004)

Edward L. Bishop, 'Pursuing "It" through "Kew Gardens" ', *Studies in Short Fiction* 19.3 (Summer 1982), pp. 269–75

Selma Meyerowitz, 'What Is to Console Us? The Politics of Deception in Woolf's Short Stories', in Jane Marcus (ed.), *New Feminist Essays on Virginia Woolf* (Lincoln: University of Nebraska Press, 1981)

Leena Kore Schröder, 'Tales of Abjection and Miscegenation: Virginia Woolf's and Leonard Woolf's "Jewish" Stories', *Twentieth Century Literature* 49.3 (Autumn 2003), pp. 298–327

Woolf's nonfiction

The key critical nonfiction works by Woolf that beginning readers should consult are, firstly, her longest work of literary criticism, *A Room of One's Own* (1929), a founding feminist text, and a major source of debate in literary criticism concerning gender, sexuality and feminism; and, secondly, her essays 'Modern Fiction' (1919, 1925) and 'Mr Bennett and Mrs Brown' (1924), which are standard texts in the field of modernist studies. Another highly influential book is *Three Guineas* (1938), her pacifist tract analysing correlations between patriarchy and fascism. Woolf published two volumes of essays in her lifetime (*The Common Reader*, first and second series; 1925 and 1932), and there have been numerous collections published posthumously. I will focus on *A Room of One's Own*, 'Modern Fiction' and 'Mr Bennett and Mrs Brown'. A selection of key essays will be discussed in brief.

A Room of One's Own (1929)

This book is enormously important, not only for readers of Woolf's work (to which it may act as an excellent introduction in its own right), but also for those interested in wider critical and cultural debates on feminism, gender, sexuality and modernity. This work is undoubtedly Woolf's most important contribution to literary criticism and theory. *A Room of One's Own* is based on lectures that Woolf gave to women students at Cambridge, but it reads in places like a novel, blurring boundaries between criticism and fiction. It is regarded as the first modern primer for feminist literary criticism, not least because it is also a source of many, often conflicting, theoretical positions.

A Room of One's Own is cited as the *locus classicus* for a number of important modern feminist debates concerning gender, sexuality, materialism, education, patriarchy, androgyny, subjectivity, the feminine sentence, the notion of 'Shakespeare's sister', the canon, the body, race, class, and so on. The title alone has had enormous impact as cultural shorthand for a modern feminist agenda. It is a very readable, and accessible, work, partly because of its playful fictional style; it introduces in this reader-friendly manner some complicated critical and theoretical issues. Many works of criticism, interpretation and theory have developed from Woolf's original points in *A Room of One's Own*. Bold type will be used to introduce the main concepts that derive from this work.

Woolf developed *A Room of One's Own* from two lectures given to Cambridge women students, and an essay version, on 'Women and Fiction'; and although much revised and expanded, the final version significantly retains the original's sense of a woman speaking to women. As part of her *experimental* fictional narrative strategy, Woolf uses shifting narrative personae to present her argument.

Writing 'I': feminist narrative strategies and subjectivity: Woolf anticipates recent theoretical concerns with the constitution of gender and subjectivity in language when she begins by declaring that ' "I" is only a convenient term for somebody who has no real being . . . (call me Mary Beton, Mary Seton, Mary Carmichael or by any name you please – it is not a matter of any importance)' (*AROO* 5). And *A Room of One's Own* is written in the voice of at least one of these Mary figures, who are to be found in the Scottish ballad 'The Four Marys'. She ventriloquises much of her argument through the voice of her own 'Mary Beton'. In the course of the book, this Mary encounters new versions of the other Marys – Mary Seton has become a student at 'Fernham' college, and Mary Carmichael an aspiring novelist – and it has been suggested that Woolf's opening and closing remarks may be in the voice of Mary Hamilton (the narrator of the ballad). *A Room of One's Own* is full of quotations from other texts, too. It is collage-like and multivocal. The allusion to the Scottish ballad feeds a subtext in Woolf's argument concerning the suppression of the role of motherhood – Mary Hamilton sings the ballad from the gallows where she is to be hung for infanticide. (Marie Carmichael, furthermore, is the *nom de plume* of contraceptive activist Marie Stopes who published a novel, *Love's Creation*, in 1928.) All these different voices make it difficult to talk about *A Room of One's Own* or indeed any other work of literature as being produced by a solitary individual. The writing self seems to be constituted in a collective of selves.

Materialism: The main argument of *A Room of One's Own*, which was titled 'Women and Fiction' in earlier drafts, is that 'a woman must have money and a room of her own if she is to write fiction' (*AROO* 4). This is a materialist argument that seems to differ from her apparent disdain for the 'materialism' of the Edwardian novelists that she records in 'Modern Fiction' and 'Mr Bennett and Mrs Brown' (see below). The narrator of *A Room of One's Own* begins by telling of her experience of visiting 'Oxbridge' university where she was refused access to the library because of her gender. She compares in some detail the splendid opulence of her lunch at a men's college with the austerity of her dinner at a more recently established women's college (Fernham). This account is the foundation for the book's main, materialist, argument: 'intellectual freedom depends upon material things' (*AROO* 141). The categorisation of middle-class women like herself with the working classes may seem problematic, but Woolf proposes, in *A Room of One's Own*, that women be understood as a separate class altogether. *A Room of One's Own* was published in the year after the full enfranchisement of women, ten years after the enfranchisement of working-class men along with middle-class, propertied women over thirty years of age.

Woolf puts forward, in *A Room of One's Own*, a sophisticated and much-quoted simile for the material basis of literary production when she begins to consider the apparent dearth of literature by women in the Elizabethan period:

> fiction is like a spider's web, attached ever so lightly perhaps, but still attached to life at all four corners. Often the attachment is scarcely perceptible; Shakespeare's plays, for instance, seem to hang there complete by themselves. But when the web is pulled askew, hooked up at the edge, torn in the middle, one remembers that these webs are not spun in mid-air by incorporeal creatures, but are the work of suffering human beings, and are attached to grossly material things, like health and money and the houses we live in.   (*AROO* 62–3)

The passage offers a number of different ways of understanding literary materialism. Firstly, it suggests that writing itself is physically made, and not divinely given or unearthly and transcendent. Woolf seems to be attempting to demystify the solitary, romantic figure of the (male) poet or author as mystically singled out, or divinely elected. But the idea that a piece of writing is a material object is also connected to a strand of modernist aesthetics concerned with texts as self-reflexive objects, and to a more general sense of the materiality of the text, the concreteness of words, spoken or printed. Secondly, the passage suggests writing as bodily process. Thirdly, writing as 'the work of suffering human beings' suggests that literature is produced as compensation for, or in protest against, existential pain and material lack. Finally, moving from this general sense of connection with human lived experience to a more specific one, in proposing writing as 'attached to grossly material things, like health and money and the houses we live in', Woolf is delineating a model of literature as grounded in the 'real world', that is, in the realms of historical, political and social experience.

Woman as reader: subjectivity and gender: After looking at the difference between men's and women's experiences of university, the narrator of *A Room of One's Own* visits the British Museum (also a significant location in *Jacob's Room*), where she researches 'Women and Poverty' under an edifice of patriarchal texts, concluding that women 'have served all these centuries as looking glasses . . . reflecting the figure of man at twice his natural size' (*AROO* 45). Here Woolf touches upon the forced, subordinate, complicity of women in the construction of the patriarchal subject. Later in the book Woolf offers a more explicit model of this when she describes the difficulties for a woman reader encountering the first-person pronoun in the novels of 'Mr A': 'a shadow seemed to lie across the page. It was a straight dark bar, a shadow shaped something like the letter "I". . . . Back one was always hailed to the letter "I". One began to tire of "I". . . . In the shadow of the letter "I" all is shapeless as mist. Is that a tree? No it is a woman' (*AROO* 130). For a man to write 'I' seems to involve the displacement of a woman in its shadow, as if women are not included as writers or users of the first-person singular in language. This displacement of the feminine in the representation and construction of subjectivity not only emphasises the alienation experienced by women readers of male-authored texts but also suggests the linguistic difficulties for women writers in trying to express feminine subjectivity when the language they have to work with seems to have already excluded them. When the word 'I' appears, the argument goes, it is always and already signifying a masculine self.

Women in history and woman as sign: The narrator of *A Room of One's Own* discovers that language, and specifically literary language, is not only capable of excluding women as its signified meaning, but also uses concepts of the feminine itself as signs. Woolf's narrator points out that there is a significant discrepancy between women in the real world and 'woman' in the symbolic order:

> Imaginatively she is of the highest importance; practically she is
> completely insignificant. She pervades poetry from cover to cover; she is

> all but absent from history. She dominates the lives of kings and
> conquerors in fiction; in fact she was the slave of any boy whose parents
> forced a ring upon her finger. Some of the most inspired words, some
> of the most profound thoughts in literature fall from her lips; in real
> life she could scarcely spell, and was the property of her
> husband.   (*AROO* 56)

Woolf here emphasises not only the relatively sparse representation of
women's experience in historical records, but also the more complicated
business of how the feminine is already caught up in the conventions of
representation itself; how women may be represented at all when 'woman', in
poetry and fiction, is already a sign, that is, a signifier in patriarchal discourse, functioning as part of the symbolic order: 'It was certainly an odd
monster that one made up by reading the historians first and the poets
afterwards – a worm winged like an eagle; the spirit of life and beauty in a
kitchen chopping suet. But these monsters, however amusing to the imagination, have no existence in fact' (*AROO* 56).

Woolf converts this dual image to a positive emblem for a feminist writing:

> What one must do to bring her to life was to think poetically and
> prosaically at one and the same moment, thus keeping in touch with
> fact – that she is Mrs Martin, aged thirty-six, dressed in blue, wearing a
> black hat and brown shoes; but not losing sight of fiction either – that
> she is a vessel in which all sorts of spirits and forces are coursing and
> flashing perpetually.   (*AROO* 56–7)

This dualistic model, contrasting prose and poetry, is of central importance to
Woolf's modernist aesthetic, encapsulated in the term 'granite and rainbow'.

Androgyny: *A Room of One's Own* can be confusing because it puts forward
contradictory sets of arguments. An important example is in her much-cited
passage on androgyny. Woolf's narrator declares that 'it is fatal for anyone
who writes to think of their sex' (*AROO* 136), and a model of writerly
androgyny is put forward, derived from Samuel Taylor Coleridge's work:

> It is fatal to be a man or woman pure and simple; one must be
> woman-manly or man-womanly. It is fatal for a woman to lay the least
> stress on any grievance; to plead even with justice any cause; in any way to
> speak consciously as a woman. And fatal is no figure of speech; for
> anything written with that conscious bias is doomed to death. It ceases to
> be fertilized. . . . Some collaboration has to take place in the mind between
> the woman and the man before the art of creation can be accomplished.
> Some marriage of opposites has to be accomplished.   (*AROO* 136)

William Shakespeare, the poet-playwright, is Woolf's ideal androgynous writer. She lists others – all men – who have also achieved androgyny: John Keats, Lawrence Sterne, William Cowper, Charles Lamb, and Marcel Proust (the only contemporary). But if the ideal is for both women and men writers to achieve androgyny, elsewhere *A Room of One's Own* puts the case for finding a language that is gendered – one appropriate for women to use when writing about women.

Gendered sentences: *A Room of One's Own* culminates in the prophesy of a woman poet to equal or rival Shakespeare – 'Shakespeare's sister'. But in collectively preparing for her appearance, women writers need to develop in several respects. In predicting that the aspiring novelist, Mary Carmichael, 'will be a poet . . . in another hundred years' time' (*AROO* 123), Mary Beton seems to be suggesting that prose must be explored and exploited in certain ways by women writers before they can be poets. She also finds fault with contemporary male writers – such as Mr A, who is 'protesting against the equality of the other sex by asserting his own superiority' (*AROO* 132). She sees this as the direct result of women's political agitation for equality: 'The Suffrage campaign was no doubt to blame' (*AROO* 129). She raises further concerns about politics and aesthetics when she comments on the aspirations of the Italian fascists for a poet worthy of fascism: 'We may well join in that pious hope, but it is doubtful whether poetry can come out of an incubator. Poetry ought to have a mother as well as a father. The Fascist poem, one may fear, will be a horrid little abortion such as one sees in a glass jar in the museum of some county town' (*AROO* 134). Yet if the extreme patriarchy of fascism cannot produce poetry because it denies a maternal line, Woolf argues that women cannot write poetry either until the historical canon of women's writing has been uncovered and acknowledged. Nineteenth-century women writers experienced great difficulty because they lacked a female tradition: 'For we think back through our mothers if we are women' (*AROO* 99). They therefore lacked literary tools suitable for expressing women's experience. The dominant sentence at the start of the nineteenth century was 'a man's sentence . . . It was a sentence that was unsuited for women's use' (*AROO* 99–100).

Woolf's assertion here, through Mary Beton, that women must write in gendered sentence structure – that is, develop a feminine syntax – and that 'the book has somehow to be adapted to the body' (*AROO* 101) seems to contradict the declaration that 'it is fatal for anyone who writes to think of their sex'. She identifies the novel as 'young enough' to be of use to the woman writer:

> No doubt we shall find her knocking that into shape for herself when she has the free use of her limbs; and providing some new vehicle, not necessarily in verse, for the poetry in her. For it is the poetry that is still the denied outlet. And I went on to ponder how a woman nowadays would write a poetic tragedy in five acts. Would she use verse? – would she not use prose rather?   (*AROO* 100–1)

Now the goal of *A Room of One's Own* has shifted from women's writing of fictional prose to poetry.

Chloe likes Olivia: So *A Room of One's Own* is concerned with what form of literary language women writers use and also what they write about. The assertion of woman as both the writing subject and the object of writing is reinforced in several places: 'above all, you must illumine your own soul' (*AROO* 117), Mary Beton advises. The 'obscure lives' (*AROO* 116) of women must be recorded by women. The example supplied is Mary Carmichael's novel, which is described as exploring women's relationships with each other. *A Room of One's Own* was published shortly after the obscenity trial provoked by Radclyffe Hall's *The Well of Loneliness* (1928), and Woolf flaunts in the face of this a blatantly lesbian narrative: 'if Chloe likes Olivia and Mary Carmichael knows how to express it she will light a torch in that vast chamber where nobody has yet been' (*AROO* 109). Her refrain, 'Chloe likes Olivia', has become a critical slogan for lesbian writing. In *A Room of One's Own*, she calls for women's writing to explore lesbianism more openly and for the narrative tools to make this possible.

The 'fine negress': One of the most controversial and contradictory passages in *A Room of One's Own* concerns Woolf's positioning of black women. Commenting on the sexual and colonial appetites of men, the narrator concludes: 'It is one of the great advantages of being a woman that one can pass even a very fine negress without wishing to make an Englishwoman of her' (*AROO* 65). In seeking to distance women from colonial practices, Woolf disturbingly excludes black women here from the very category of women. This has become the crux of much contemporary feminist debate concerning the politics of identity. The category of women both unites and divides feminists: white middle-class feminists, it has been shown, cannot speak for the experience of all women; and reconciliation of universalism and difference remains a key issue. 'Women – but are you not sick to death of the word?' Woolf retorts in the closing pages of *A Room of One's Own*. 'I can assure you I am' (*AROO* 145). The category of women is not chosen by women, it represents the space in patriarchy from which women must speak and which they struggle to redefine.

Shakespeare's sister: Another contradictory concept in *A Room of One's Own* is 'Shakespeare's sister', that is, the possibility that there will be a woman writer to match the status of Shakespeare, who has come to personify literature itself. 'Judith Shakespeare' stands for the silenced woman writer or artist. But to seek to mimic *the* model of the individual masculine writing subject may also be considered part of a conservative feminist agenda. On the other hand, Woolf seems to defer the arrival of Shakespeare's sister in a celebration of women's collective literary achievement 'I am talking of the common life which is the real life and not of the little separate lives which we live as individuals' (*AROO* 148–9). Shakespeare's sister is a messianic figure who 'lives in you and in me' (*AROO* 148) and who will draw 'her life from the lives of the unknown who were her forerunners' (*AROO* 149), but has yet to appear. She may be the common writer to Woolf's 'common reader' (a term she borrows from Samuel Johnson), but she has yet to 'put on the body which she has so often laid down' (*AROO* 149). *A Room of One's Own* closes with this contradictory model of individual achievement and collective effort. The sense of a collective authorial voice, here, in the preparations for the coming of Shakespeare's sister, is implicit in the very multivocal narrative of *A Room of One's Own*.

Suggested further reading

Michèle Barrett, 'Introduction', in Barrett (ed.), *Virginia Woolf: Women and Writing* (London: Women's Press, 1979)

Jane Marcus, 'A Very Fine Negress', in Marcus, *Hearts of Darkness: White Women Write Race* (New Brunswick, NJ: Rutgers University Press, 2004)

Toril Moi, 'Introduction', in Moi, *Sexual/Textual Politics: Feminist Literary Theory* (London: Methuen, 1985)

'Modern Fiction' (1919, 1925)

'Modern Fiction' was first published in the *Times Literary Supplement* in April 1919 as 'Modern Novels'. This was revised for Woolf's first collection of essays, the first *The Common Reader* (1925). It is Woolf's most well-known and most frequently quoted essay. It is, along with T. S. Eliot's 'Tradition and the Individual Talent' and Ezra Pound's 'A Retrospect', one of the main manifestos examined in the study of literary modernism. It is also an important source for readers seeking to understand Woolf's own writing methods.

Woolf distinguishes in this essay between what she calls the old-fashioned and outmoded 'materialism' of the Edwardian novelists, such as Arnold

Bennett, John Galsworthy and H. G. Wells, and the more modern, 'spiritual' and experimental writing of her Georgian contemporaries, and in particular the work of James Joyce. She argues that Bennett's writing is ruled by plot and characterisation. He is obliged 'to provide comedy, tragedy, love interest, and an air of probability embalming the whole so impeccable that if all his figures were to come to life they would find themselves dressed down to the last button of their coats in the fashion of the hour' (*E4* 160). Such writing, Woolf argues, for all its obsession with material detail, fails to capture 'life'. She explains this in a passage that is probably her most famous and most quoted passage of literary criticism: 'Look within and life, it seems, is very far from being "like this". Examine for a moment an ordinary mind on an ordinary day. The mind receives a myriad impressions – trivial, fantastic, evanescent, or engraved with the sharpness of steel' (*E4* 160).

Woolf is putting forward a model of the writer's mind as an 'ordinary' one, and one that is best understood as a blank sheet of paper, which absorbs mental impressions from the data of the outside world. She continues:

> From all sides they come, an incessant shower of innumerable atoms; and as they fall, as they shape themselves into the life of Monday or Tuesday, the accent falls differently from of old; the moment of importance came not here but there; so that, if a writer were a free man and not a slave, if he could write what he chose, not what he must, if he could base his work not upon convention, there would be no plot, no comedy, no love interest or catastrophe in the accepted style, and perhaps not a single button sewn on as the Bond Street tailors would have it. (*E4* 160)

In this model of writing, the writer has somehow to convey such mental impressions without worrying about representing external material detail as if from the outside. Woolf is concerned with what happens to the writer's mind when it processes such information, that is with the inner life, as it is experienced. She uses a striking set of luminous images to express this:

> Life is not a series of gig lamps symmetrically arranged; life is a luminous halo, a semi-transparent envelope surrounding us from the beginning of consciousness to the end. Is it not the task of the novelist to convey this varying, this unknown and uncircumscribed spirit, whatever aberration or complexity it may display, with as little mixture of the alien and external as possible? (*E4* 160–1)

Woolf is suggesting that novelists must be true to this inner process in order to capture properly what life really is. She continues with a description of the mind as if it is blotting paper: 'Let us record the atoms as they fall upon the mind in the order in which they fall, let us trace the pattern, however disconnected and incoherent in appearance, which each sight scores upon the consciousness. Let us not take for granted that life exists more fully in what is commonly thought big than is commonly thought small' (*E4* 161).

Woolf argues for this subjective, fleeting, interior experience as the proper stuff of fiction, and she recommends the abandonment of conventional plot, genre and narrative structure. The interior qualities she is describing are very like the narrative form known as 'stream-of-consciousness', and this is the method that Joyce perfected in the work that Woolf focuses on in her essay. She talks about his *A Portrait of the Artist as a Young Man* (1916) and extracts from *Ulysses* (1922) as examples of the new 'spiritual' writing. Joyce, she argues, is 'concerned at all costs to reveal the flickerings of that inmost flame which flashes its messages through the brain' (*E4* 161). Woolf's interest in how Joyce conveys moments in time as subjective experience and the reception of a flow of images, experiences and emotions, has something in common with the philosophy of Henri Bergson. Her 'luminous halo' image also echoes an image from Joseph Conrad's *Heart of Darkness* (1902). But although Woolf talks about Joyce's great work, *Ulysses*, as a 'masterpiece' and admires 'its brilliancy, its sordidity, its incoherence, its sudden lightning flashes of significance', she does strike a more negative note in saying that it 'fails to compare' with the work of Joseph Conrad or Thomas Hardy 'because of the comparative poverty of the writer's mind' (161). But 'Modern Fiction' is an important and early defence of his work, and from this has been understood more broadly as a manifesto of modernism.

But there is more to the essay than its most famous passage, which is a meditation mainly on *Joyce's* new fictional methods. Woolf's own 'method' in the essay is to question Joyce's method as much as she questions Bennett's. If Bennett's materialism is lacking, so ultimately is Joyce's 'spiritual' method. She also looks in the essay at the 'influence' of the Russian writers, and of Chekhov in particular. Sympathetic with all these approaches, she nevertheless exposes their limitations. She also sees something in the tradition of English literature that is missing from the Russian:

> But perhaps we see something that escapes them, or why should this voice of protest mix itself with our gloom? The voice of protest is the voice of another and an ancient civilisation which seems to have bred in us the instinct to enjoy and fight rather than to suffer and understand. English fiction from Sterne to Meredith bears witness to our natural delight in humour and comedy, in the beauty of earth, in the activities of the intellect, and in the splendour of the body. (*E4* 163)

Here Woolf is outlining a distinctly English tradition of dissent, rationalism, humour, materialism, pleasure and sensuousness. But the essay closes by finding that 'nothing – no "method", no experiment, even of the wildest – is forbidden, but only falsity and pretence. "The proper stuff of fiction" does not exist; everything is the proper stuff of fiction, every feeling, every thought; every quality of brain and spirit is drawn upon; no perception comes amiss' (*E4* 163–4). Woolf does not put forward just one credo for writing fiction, but rather celebrates 'the infinite possibilities of the art', and the experimentalism of her modern colleagues.

'Mr Bennett and Mrs Brown' (1924)

'Mr Bennett and Mrs Brown' was first published in the *Criterion* of July 1924, as 'Character in Fiction', and evolved from a speech to the Cambridge Heretics Society. Many of its rhetorical features survive into the published text. Here Woolf continues her assault on the Edwardians – Arnold Bennett, John Galsworthy and H. G. Wells – for their materialist conventions, and her uneven defence of the Georgians – T. S. Eliot, E. M. Forster, James Joyce, D. H. Lawrence and Lytton Strachey – whose work, she declares, must make us 'reconcile ourselves to a season of failures and fragments' (*E3* 435).

    The essay's title is derived from its central, virtuoso conceit whereby Woolf illustrates the inadequacies of the Edwardian novelists as she makes a number of attempts, using their materialist 'tools', to construct a fictional narrative about the character of 'Mrs Brown', a stranger encountered on a train:

> As I sat down I had the strange and uncomfortable feeling that I was interrupting a conversation between two people who were already sitting there. Not that they were young or happy. Far from it. They were both elderly, the woman over sixty, the man well over forty. They were sitting opposite each other, and the man, who had been leaning over and talking emphatically to judge by his attitude and the flush on his face, sat back and became silent. I had disturbed him, and he was annoyed. The elderly lady, however, whom I will call Mrs Brown, seemed rather relieved.   (*E3* 423)

She calls the man Mr Smith. Overhearing their conversation, the narrator concludes: 'It was plain, from Mrs Brown's silence, from the uneasy affability with which Mr Smith spoke, that he had some power over her which he was exerting disagreeably.' After further exchanges Mr Smith 'jumped out of the train before it had stopped at Clapham Junction' (*E3* 424) and the narrator is left alone with Mrs Brown, and begins to imagine all sorts of details about her.

The point of this anecdote is to show how 'a character impos[es] itself upon another person. Here is Mrs Brown making someone begin almost automatically to write a novel about her. I believe that all novels begin with an old lady in the corner opposite' (*E3* 425). If novels are concerned with the expression of character, Woolf proposes that this expression varies

> according to the age and country in which you happen to be born. It would be easy enough to write three different versions of that incident in the train, an English, a French, and a Russian. The English writer would make the old lady into a "character"; he would bring out her oddities and mannerisms; her buttons and wrinkles; her ribbons and warts. Her personality would dominate the book. A French writer would rub out all that; he would sacrifice the individual Mrs Brown to give a more general view of human nature; to make a more abstract, proportioned, and harmonious whole. The Russian would pierce through the flesh; would reveal the soul – the soul alone, wandering out into the Waterloo Road, asking of life some tremendous question which would sound on and on in our ears after the book was finished.   (*E3* 426)

Woolf pursues the characterisation of Mrs Brown in order to argue with her literary rival, Bennett, about the achievements of modern novelists, who, he says, fail 'because they cannot create characters who are real, true, and convincing' (*E3* 427). Woolf puts the ball back in Bennett's court by suggesting that he and his contemporaries, Wells and Galsworthy, have themselves failed to provide adequate examples to follow: 'Now it seems to me that to go to these men and ask them to teach you how to write a novel – how to create characters that are real – is precisely like going to a boot maker and asking him to teach you how to make a watch' (*E3* 427). Woolf then gets us to imagine how these writers would treat Mrs Brown if they were travelling to Waterloo with her:

> Seizing upon all these symptoms of the unsatisfactory condition of our primary schools with a rapidity to which I can do no justice, Mr Wells would instantly project upon the window-pane a vision of a better, breezier, jollier, happier, more adventurous and gallant world, where these musty railway carriages and fusty old women do not exist; where miraculous barges bring tropical fruit to Camberwell by eight o'clock in the morning; where there are public nurseries, fountains, and libraries, dining-rooms, drawing-rooms, and marriages; where every citizen is generous and candid, manly and magnificent, and rather like Mr Wells himself. But nobody is in the least like Mrs Brown.   (*E3* 428)

Galsworthy would take a different approach:

> Can we doubt that the walls of Doulton's factory would take his fancy?
> There are women in that factory who make twenty-five dozen
> earthenware pots every day. There are mothers in the Mile End Road
> who depend upon the farthings which those women earn. But there are
> employers in Surrey who are even now smoking rich cigars while the
> nightingale sings. Burning with indignation, stuffed with information,
> arraigning civilization, Mr Galsworthy would only see in Mrs Brown a
> pot broken on the wheel and thrown into the corner.   (*E3* 428)

Finally, the technique of Bennett himself is imagined:

> Mr Bennett, alone of the Edwardians, would keep his eyes in the
> carriage. He, indeed, would observe every detail with immense care. He
> would notice the advertisements; the pictures of Swanage and
> Portsmouth; the way in which the cushion bulged between the buttons;
> how Mrs Brown wore a brooch which had cost three-and-ten-three at
> Whitworth's bazaar; and had mended both gloves – indeed the thumb
> of the left-hand glove had been replaced.   (*E3* 428)

Woolf then turns to a detailed analysis of Bennett's own writing in his novel
Hilda Lessways (1911), to enforce her critique. Instead of hearing the voices
of his characters, she maintains:

> we can only hear Mr Bennett's voice telling us facts about rents and
> freeholds and copyholds and fines. What can Mr Bennett be about?
> I have formed my own opinion of what Mr Bennett is about – he is
> trying to make us imagine for him; he is trying to hypnotize us into the
> belief that, because he has made a house, there must be a person living
> there. With all his powers of observation, which are marvellous, with all
> his sympathy and humanity, which are great, Mr Bennett has never once
> looked at Mrs Brown in her corner.   (*E3* 430)

Mrs Brown has become 'eternal' and the symbol of 'human nature' in
Woolf's argument. She 'changes only on the surface, it is the novelists who get
in and out – there she sits and not one of the Edwardian writers has so much
as looked at her' (*E3* 430). Woolf maintains that the Edwardian writers 'have
laid an enormous stress upon the fabric of things. They have given us a house
in the hope that we may be able to deduce the human beings who live there.
Therefore, you see, the Georgian writer had to begin by throwing away the
method that was in use at the moment' (*E3* 432). Woolf describes this
Georgian rejection of Edwardian tools in terms of violence:

at whatever cost of life, limb, and damage to valuable property
Mrs Brown must be rescued, expressed, and set in her high relations to
the world before the train stopped and she disappeared for ever. And
so the smashing and the crashing began. Thus it is that we hear all
round us, in poems and novels and biographies, even in newspaper
articles and essays, the sound of breaking and falling, crashing and
destruction. It is the prevailing sound of the Georgian age.   (*E3* 433–4)

It is as if the train Mrs Brown is travelling on is hurtling towards a cata-
strophic accident. The impact of the dissonant, unnerving style of the new
writers such as Eliot, Forster, Joyce, Lawrence and Strachey is communicated.
It is in this context, of the bumpy transition from Edwardian to Georgian,
that Woolf's argument about change in human character is made.

The essay maintains on the one hand that Mrs Brown is 'eternal' and
unchanging, but on the other hand, it famously asserts that 'on or about
December 1910 human character changed' (*E3* 421). This has come to
represent for many cultural commentators the cataclysmic moment of modernity, the inception of the avant-garde, the shock of the new (see Chapter
Two). In the context of the essay, it marks the shift from the Edwardian to the
Georgian era, when 'all human relations have shifted – those between masters
and servants, husbands and wives, parents and children. And when human
relations change there is at the same time a change in religion, conduct,
politics, and literature' (*E3* 422). In general, Woolf is not arguing that
literature merely changes in terms of subject matter to *reflect* new, modern,
experience, but that literary form itself undergoes radical, and turbulent,
transformation: 'And so the smashing and the crashing began. . . . Grammar
is violated; syntax disintegrated' (*E3* 434). The work of Joyce, Eliot and
Strachey illustrates the point that modern literature has necessarily become
caught up in the business of finding new form. By 1924, when the essay
appeared, Joyce's *Ulysses* had been published as a book, in the same year as
Eliot's *The Waste Land*. Readers must 'tolerate the spasmodic, the obscure,
the fragmentary, the failure' (*E3* 436). The self-reflexive, fragmentary, subjective and momentary qualities of modernist writing are here acknowledged
and celebrated.

Suggested further reading
Rachel Bowlby, *Feminist Destinations and Further Essays on Virginia Woolf*
   (Edinburgh: Edinburgh University Press, 1997)
Randall Stevenson, *Modernist Fiction: An Introduction*, rev. edn (London: Prentice
   Hall, 1998)

Three Guineas (1938)

Whereas *A Room of One's Own* is centred in literary criticism, analysing and probing the production of literature by and about women, *Three Guineas* focuses on the political and social institutions of patriarchy and connects the politics of the rising fascism in Europe with the politics of the personal and domestic sphere at home. Woolf declares women to have 'outsider status', and she more radically separates off the category of women as, paradoxically, transcending all boundaries, including national ones: 'As a woman, I have no country. As a woman I want no country. As a woman my country is the whole world' (*TG* 313).

Three Guineas is in three chapters. In the first, Woolf attempts to answer the question 'How are we to prevent war?' (*TG* 4), a question that leads her directly to the politics of gender, and to the material basis for women's economic independence and education. Only by escaping domestic tyranny through the offices of formal education can women begin to prevent war. Chapter Two addresses the need for women to become economically independent, if they are to prevent war, and considers the contradictions inherent in women's entry into the professions. Chapter Three explores the irony of a woman's being asked to sign a manifesto to preserve 'culture and intellectual liberty', when women have been systematically denied access to both. Each chapter debates the merits of spending a guinea on a different cause. There are five photographs illustrating the argument, and an ample set of supporting notes and references.

Chapter One begins by explaining that the narrator has been approached by a barrister asking: 'How in your opinion are we to prevent war?' His question opens up a 'gulf so deeply cut between' himself and his addressee because of their difference in sex. The education of men has been at the expense of the education of women, so women are not equipped to respond as men might. Woolf invokes William Makepeace Thackery's phrase, 'Arthur's Education Fund' ('AEF'), to explain the sacrifice that the daughters of educated men have traditionally made for their brothers. She ascribes the instinct to kill to men, and detects a pleasure, 'some glory, some necessity, some satisfaction' in fighting (*TG* 39). Although there are exceptions, such as Wilfred Owen, the majority of men are motivated to warfare by patriotism. Woolf refers us to the photographs dominating the press at the time of the dead bodies and ruined houses that were the result of the fascist bombing in the Spanish Civil War. Such images press the case that 'War must be stopped at whatever cost' (*TG* 11). The narrator's correspondent has urged her to sign a petition, join his society and make a donation to it. Woolf is moved by these requests to consider what powers and influence daughters of educated men possess. She considers, too, 'the sartorial splendours of the educated man' when she turns to the official positions occupied by men to the exclusion of women. And she concludes that before women are in a position to prevent war, they must be properly funded in education. The narrator of *Three Guineas* duly donates her first guinea to the funding of a women's university college.

Chapter Two turns from education to professional life, and the narrator considers a request for donations to a fund to assist women into the professions. Here Woolf makes explicit her linking of fascist and Nazi politics with domestic tyranny. She quotes misogynist statements uttered by British men and reported in the *Daily Telegraph* alongside similar sentiments uttered by German Nazis. She asks: 'Are they not both the voices of Dictators, whether they speak English or German, and are we not all agreed that the dictator when we meet him abroad is a very dangerous as well as a very ugly animal?' (*TG* 97). She argues that women are already fighting dictatorship in the private, domestic sphere: 'Should we not help her to crush him in our own country before we ask her to help us crush him abroad?' (*TG* 98). The narrator's second guinea therefore goes to 'help the daughters of uneducated women to enter the professions', and it is given with the proviso that the beneficiaries help 'to prevent war' (*TG* 152).

Chapter Three confronts the barrister's request to sign the manifesto for the protection of 'culture and intellectual liberty' with the fact of 'Arthur's Education Fund', evidence of women's continuing and enforced support of these freedoms for men at the expense of their own. Woolf puts forward the proposal for an 'anonymous and secret Society of Outsiders', one that would have no officials or meetings, and be dedicated to peace and progressive life in the professions and education. She likens the foreign and domestic dictators to the tyrant Creon in Sophocles' *Antigone*. She shows that there are women already at work in society, like Antigone, undermining such dictatorships. Declining to sign the petition or to join her correspondent's society, the narrator concludes by donating her third guinea to the barrister's pacifist cause, underlining that her first two guineas donated to women's causes are in themselves donations to this common cause: 'the rights of all – all men and women – to respect their persons of the great principles of Justice and Equality and Liberty' (*TG* 260–1). The three guineas, then, 'though given to three different treasurers are all given to the same cause' (*TG* 361). Woolf's pacifist tract argues for the economic and material grounds to promote women in education and the professions, achievements that feed into the common goal of preventing war. Her invocation of Sophocles' *Antigone* underpins her understanding of such feminist projects as in keeping with rationalist, humanist, Enlightenment traditions. When the word feminism is redundant, so, too, will be dictatorship.

Suggested further reading

Berenice A. Caroll, ' "To Crush Him in our Own Country": The Political Thought of Virginia Woolf', *Feminist Studies* 4.1 (1978), pp. 99–131

Elena Gualtieri, '*Three Guineas* and the Photograph: the Art of Propaganda', in Maroula Joannon (ed.), *Women Writers of the 1930s: Gender, Politics and History* (Edinburgh: Edinburgh University Press, 1999)

Anna Snaith, 'Wide Circles: the *Three Guineas* Letters', *Woolf Studies Annual* 6 (2000), pp. 1–12

Other essays

Virginia Woolf wrote numerous essays, articles and reviews. She published two volumes of essays, *The Common Reader* (1925) and *The Common Reader: Second Series* (1932), and several collections have appeared posthumously. Some of her key essays include 'Romance and the Heart' (1923), 'On Not Knowing Greek' (1925), 'Poetry, Fiction and the Future' (1927), 'Street Haunting: A London Adventure' (1927), 'Professions for Women' (1931), 'Memories of a Working Women's Guild' (1931), 'Craftsmanship' (1937), 'The Leaning Tower' (1940), and 'Thoughts on Peace in an Air Raid' (1940).

Woolf puts forward a theory of gendered aesthetic form in **'Romance and the Heart'** (1923), her review of Dorothy Richardson's novel *Revolving Lights* (1923). According to Woolf, Richardson 'has invented, or, if she has not invented, developed and applied to her own uses, a sentence which we might call the psychological sentence of the feminine gender. It is of a more elastic fibre than the old, capable of stretching to the extreme, of suspending the frailest particles, of enveloping the vaguest shapes' (*E3* 367). But, acknowledging that men, too, have constructed similar sentences, she points out that the difference lies with content rather than form:

> Miss Richardson has fashioned her sentence consciously, in order that it may descend to the depths and investigate the crannies of Miriam Henderson's consciousness. It is a woman's sentence only in the sense that it is used to describe a woman's mind by a writer who is neither proud nor afraid of anything that she may discover in the psychology of her sex. (*E* 367)

Woolf is emphasising that Richardson's achievement is in mapping previously unrecorded experiences of women. She has constructed sentences whose form enables this process of inscription.

Woolf wrote **'On Not Knowing Greek'** (1925) specifically for her collection *The Common Reader*, and she embarked on a programme of over two years of reading and translating classical Greek texts in preparation for it. She read Plato, Homer, Sophocles, Euripides and Aristophanes, and made her own translation of Aeschylus' *Agamemnon* (which is now in the Berg archive, New York). The detailed knowledge of Greek texts displayed in the essay belies its title, but Woolf's point is that we cannot know or experience Greek literature in the way the ancient Greeks themselves did. In her essay she contrasts the English landscape with the Greek and emphasises the alien nature of the latter, to which the former can never approximate:

> It is the climate that is impossible. If we try to think of Sophocles here, we must annihilate the smoke and the damp and the thick wet mists. We must sharpen the lines of the hills. We must imagine a beauty of stone and earth rather than of woods and greenery. With warmth and sunshine and months of brilliant, fine weather, life of course is instantly changed. (*E4* 39–40)

The landscape and climate, integral to the drama, mark out the gulf between the cultures, as Woolf understands it: 'They were speaking to an enormous audience rayed round them on one of those brilliant southern days when the sun is so hot and yet the air so exciting' (*E4* 40). She speaks of the directness, the 'sharpness and compression' (*E4* 42) of these plays as a lost ideal, but one that despite the English landscape and weather, may nevertheless be understood as standing at the root of English culture: 'the stable, the permanent, the original human being is to be found there . . . These are the originals, Chaucer's the varieties of the human species' (*E4* 42).

This concern with classical Greek origins is in keeping with that of other modernist writers such as T. S. Eliot, James Joyce and Ezra Pound. Woolf uses the differences in climate as an analogy for the loss of literary directness; it is as if the 'thick wet mists' of England have clouded over the Greeks' sun. Centuries of lesser imitations have obscured the splendour of the originals and turned them into 'the greatest bores and the most demoralising companions in the world. The plays of Addison, Voltaire, and a host of others are there to prove it' (*E4* 42). In order to feel the benefit of the sun, we must 'encounter [the plays] in the Greek':

> A fragment of their speech broken off would, we feel, colour oceans
> and oceans of the respectable drama. Here we meet them before their
> emotions have been worn into uniformity. Here we listen to the
> nightingale whose song echoes through English literature singing in
> her own Greek tongue. For the first time Orpheus with his lute makes
> men and beasts follow him. Their voices ring out clear and sharp; we
> see the hairy, tawny bodies at play in the sunlight among the trees,
> not posed gracefully on granite plinths in the pale corridors of the
> British Museum.   (*E4* 42)

Reading classical Greek in the original language rather than translation does
something to restore the lost directness, and Woolf talks of the tonic effects of
doing so: 'It is to the Greeks that we turn when we are sick of the vagueness,
of the confusion, of the Christianity and its consolations, of our own age'
(*E4* 51). In this, one of her most significant essays, Woolf is celebrating
pre-Christian and rationalist, Enlightenment sources for her philosophy
and her aesthetics.

In the essay **'Poetry, Fiction and the Future'** (1927; also known as 'The
Narrow Bridge of Art'), Woolf acknowledges the different tasks each genre
traditionally performs, but is interested in creating a new form of writing that
marries prose and poetry: '[Poetry] has always insisted on certain rights, such
as rhyme, metre, poetic diction. She has never been used for the common
purpose of life. Prose has taken all the dirty work on to her own shoulders;
has answered letters, paid bills, written articles, made speeches, served the
needs of business men, shopkeepers, lawyers, soldiers, peasants' (*E4* 434).
Woolf's personification of poetry as a militant 'insist[ing] on certain rights'
suggests a politicisation of poetics, but she makes us reread poetry as an
aristocrat clinging to certain traditional privileges when she personifies prose
as a servant taking on 'all the dirty work'. She anticipates a new form of
writing in a 'prose which has many of the characteristics of poetry', asking
whether prose can 'chant the elegy, or hymn the love, or shriek in terror, or
praise the rose' (*E4* 436), and so on. This is a celebration of the new lyrical
prose of modernism – and indeed of her own novel, *To the Lighthouse* (1927),
which she termed an elegy (*D3* 34); and it is imbued with the rhetoric of class
war: the domain of (courtly) love poetry is to be opened to and transformed
by the stevedore of prose.

'Street Haunting: A London Adventure' (1927) is one of Woolf's many
scintillating attempts at conveying the experience of city life. It describes 'the
greatest pleasure of town life in winter – rambling the streets of London' (*E4*
480). The narrator, who is in the tradition of a modernist *flâneur*, a tradition
described as democratic in that it is carried on by a 'vast republican army of

anonymous trampers' (*E4* 481), embarks on a journey, ostensibly to buy a pencil, and in the 'fine evening' light encounters a number of scenes. She communicates the pleasures of merely looking: 'Let us . . . be content still with surfaces – the glossy brilliance of the motor omnibuses; the carnal splendour of the butchers' shops with their yellow flanks and their purple steaks; the blue and red bunches of flowers burning so bravely through the plate glass of the florists' windows' (*E4* 482). A 'dwarf' accompanied by 'giantesses' is empathetically described trying on shoes (*E4* 483), and back out in the street the narrator observes the 'maimed company of the halt and the blind', commenting on 'a bearded Jew, wild, hunger-bitten' and 'the humped body of an old woman flung abandoned on the step of a public building' (*E4* 484). These 'derelict' figures are juxtaposed against the more prosperous 'diners and dancers' enjoying theatres and restaurants (*E4* 484).

Having paused at a bookshop, and then eventually bought a pencil in another place, the narrator returns, musing on the alternative selves that the streets make available: 'One could become a washerwoman, a publican, a street singer. And what greater delight and wonder can there be than to leave the straight lines of personality and deviate into those footpaths that lead beneath brambles and thick tree trunks into the heart of the forest where live those wild beasts, our fellow men?' (*E4* 486). Woolf's pastoral imagery here encourages us to read the essay's stroll through London as an allegory on human relations and politics.

In her key feminist essay, **'Professions for Women'** (1931), a paper she read to the National Society for Women's Service, Woolf insists on the woman writer's necessary suppression of a traditionally submissive – and domestic – feminine role, encapsulated in Coventry Patmore's 'The Angel in the House'. 'The Angel in the House' personifies, then, the submissive patriarchal woman:

> She was intensely sympathetic. She was immensely charming. She was utterly unselfish. She excelled in the difficult arts of family life. If there was chicken, she took the leg; if there was a draught she sat in it – in short she was so constituted that she never had a mind or a wish of her own, but preferred to sympathize always with the minds and wishes of others.   (*CE2* 285)

As a writer, the narrator discovers that when 'the shadow of her wings fell on my page' (*CE2* 285), she rendered, with her total lack of independent thought, the art of reviewing impossible:

> Had I not killed her she would have killed me. She would have plucked the heart out of my writing. For, as I found, directly I put pen to paper, you cannot review even a novel without a mind of your own . . . Thus, whenever I felt the shadow of her wing or the radiance of her halo upon my page, I took up the inkpot and flung it at her. She died hard.   (*CE2* 286)

The struggle to suppress this phantom is something that every woman writer must endure: 'Killing the Angel in the House was part of the occupation of a woman writer' (*CE2* 286).

The paper closes with Woolf's acknowledgement that women have made, by 1931, some significant material gains. She returns to her central feminist metaphor when she remarks that the women in her audience 'have won rooms of your own in the house hitherto exclusively owned by men. You are able, though not without great labour and effort, to pay the rent. You are earning your five hundred pounds a year' (*CE2* 289). These are the material conditions that Woolf put forward, in *A Room of One's Own* (1929), as necessary for women writers to flourish. But, she warns here:

> this freedom is only a beginning; the room is your own, but it is still bare. It has to be furnished; it has to be decorated; it has to be shared. How are you going to furnish it, how are you going to decorate it? With whom are you going to share it, and upon what terms? These, I think are questions of the utmost importance and interest. For the first time in history you are able to ask them; for the first time you are able to decide for yourselves what the answers should be.   (*CE2* 289)

The material conditions for women writers extend to other professional women, and vice versa. As a writer, Woolf is aligning herself with other women who work. 'The Angel in the House' represents those women still performing the unpaid work and enforced domestic servitude of wife and mother. She is the spectre that haunts all working women.

In **'Memories of a Working Women's Guild'** (1931), Woolf explores the complexities of her position as an educated and privileged middle-class woman aligned with working-class women in organised feminist politics. It was written as an introduction to *Life As We Have Known It*, a collection of pieces by former members of the Women's Co-operative Guild (in which Woolf herself had been active). Woolf begins by recalling her initial private reservations about her Guild colleague Margaret Llewellyn-Davies's request for the very article she is now writing. Thinking back to a 1913 conference in Newcastle where in 'a public hall hung with banners and loud voices' (*LAW* xxiii) she heard working-class women speakers demand 'divorce, education, the vote – all good things . . . higher wages and shorter hours' (*LAW* xviii), she marks the difference in perspective she derives from the material benefits of class difference: 'If every reform they demand was granted this very instant it would not touch one hair of my comfortable capitalistic head. Hence my interest is merely altruistic . . . I am a benevolent spectator' (*LAW* xviii-xix). She also recalls her sense of futility, since at the time 'among all those women who worked, who bore children, who scrubbed and cooked and bargained, there was not a single woman with a vote' (*LAW* xix).

The Women's Co-Operative Guild was a powerful force for working-class women, and Woolf describes, in somewhat patronising terms, the gulf she initially felt between those women still fighting for material welfare and those like herself who can afford to pursue high culture. She shifts her focus to the head office of the Guild in Hampstead: 'Miss Kidd sat at her typewriter in the outer office. Miss Kidd, one felt, had set herself as a kind of watch-dog to ward off the meddlesome middle-class wasters of time who come prying into other people's business' (*LAW* xxiv). She goes on to explore the letters that comprise *Life As We Have Known It*, concluding: 'These pages are only fragments. These voices are beginning only now to emerge from silence into half articulate speech. These lives are still half hidden in profound obscurity' (*LAW* xxxix). These women, it appears, have begun to fulfil Woolf's injunction, in *A Room of One's Own*, to 'illumine your own soul' (*AROO* 135). Woolf closes with the example of Miss Kidd, the guild's secretary, and quotes her 'fragment of a letter':

> 'When I was a girl of seventeen,' she writes, 'my then employer, a gentleman of good position and high standing in the town, sent me to his home one night, ostensibly to take a parcel of books, but really with a very different object. When I arrived at the house all the family were away, and before he would allow me to leave he forced me to yield to him. At eighteen I was a mother.'

Woolf does not 'presume to say' whether such writing 'is literature or not literature . . . but that it explains much and reveals much is certain. Such then was the burden that rested on that sombre figure as she sat typing your letters, such were the memories she brooded as she guarded your door with her grim and indomitable fidelity' (*LAW* xxxviii–xxxix). This essay shows Woolf's awareness of the class issues that confront feminism, and it also puts into practice her espousal of a collective, multivocal women's writing.

'Craftsmanship' (1937) was written for the BBC radio series 'Words Fail Me', and Woolf read it in a broadcast on 29 April 1937 (a recording of which survives in the National Sound Archive of the British Library). In it Woolf gives a virtuoso display of verbal craftsmanship and wit, firstly by questioning the very title she has been allotted: 'to talk of craft in connection with words is to bring together two incongruous ideas', she explains, since the word '"craft" has two meanings . . . in the first place making useful objects out of solid matter' and 'in the second place, the word "craft" means cajolery, cunning, deceit' (*CE2* 245). So if these two meanings

> mate [they] can only give birth to some monster fit for a glass case in a
> museum. Instantly, therefore, the title of the talk must be changed,
> and for it substituted another – A Ramble round Words, perhaps. For
> when you cut off the head of a talk it behaves like a hen that has been
> decapitated. It runs round in a circle till it drops dead – so people say
> who have killed hens. And that must be the course, or circle, of this
> decapitated talk.   (*CE* 245)

The decaptitated hen, standing for the body of a text cut off from its title, wittily illustrates that any sample of language depends on its relation to another in order to create meaning; the erratic behaviour of the decapitated hen serves to illustrate the many directions in meaning in which any piece of language is capable of running. Language is multivalent and generates meaning by means of difference from itself.

Woolf then makes verbal sport with samples of found language – words visible, for example, to passengers on the London underground and the railway:

> We say over and over again as we pace, 'Passing Russell Square, passing
> Russell Square.' And then as we say them, the words shuffle and change,
> and we find ourselves saying, 'Passing away saith the world, passing
> away . . . The leaves decay and fall, the vapours weep their burthen to
> the ground. Man comes . . .' And then we wake up and find ourselves at
> King's Cross. (*CE2* 245–6)

Even simple informational signs to urban travellers are capable of generating endless semantic games. Woolf celebrates language as a living organism:

> words do not live in dictionaries; they live in the mind . . . And how do
> they live in the mind? Variously and strangely, much as human beings
> live, by ranging hither and thither, by falling in love, and mating
> together. It is true that they are much less bound by ceremony and
> convention than we are. Royal words mate with commoners. English
> words marry French words, German words, Indian words, Negro words,
> if they have a fancy. Indeed, the less we enquire into the past of our dear

> Mother English the better it will be for that lady's reputation. For she
> has gone a-roving, a-roving fair maid. (*CE2* 250)

It is the libertarian, transgressive and mutational powers of language that
Woolf celebrates here: 'to lay down any laws for such irreclaimable vagabonds
is worse than useless. A few trifling rules of grammar and spelling are all the
constraint we can put on them' (*CE2* 250). She is endorsing the concept of
living language as an international democratic force, something that ignores
and spills over political, national, class and racial boundaries.

Woolf wrote **'The Leaning Tower'** (1940) as a lecture, which she gave to
the Workers' Educational Association in April 1940. It is her most sustained
argument on the relationship of literature to class. She argues that until the
twentieth-century literature has been written by the middle class:

> It is a fact . . . that all writers from Chaucer to the present day, with so few
> exceptions that one hand can count them, have sat upon the same kind of
> chair – a raised chair. They have all come from the middle class; they
> have had good, at least expensive, educations. They have all been raised
> above the mass of people upon a tower of stucco – that is their middle-
> class birth; and of gold – that is their expensive education. That was
> true of all the nineteenth-century writers, save Dickens; it was true of all
> the 1914 writers, save D. H. Lawrence.   (*CE2* 168)

The privileges of material comfort and education mark out the successful
writer:

> a writer has to be taught. . . . Almost every writer who has practised his
> art successfully had been taught it. He had been taught it by about
> eleven years of education – at private schools, public schools, and
> universities. He sits upon a tower raised above the rest of us; a tower
> built first on his parents' station, then on his parents' gold. It is a tower
> of the utmost importance; it decides his angle of vision; it affects his
> power of communication.   (*CE2* 169)

Woolf identifies this position of middle-class privilege as the status quo
until the advent of the Great War, which she describes as coming 'suddenly,
like a chasm in a smooth road' (*CE2* 167). Before the war and

> all through the nineteenth century, down to August 1914, that tower
> was a steady tower. The writer was scarcely conscious either of his high
> station or of his limited vision. Many of them had sympathy, great
> sympathy, with other classes; they wished to help the working class
> to enjoy the advantages of the tower class; but they did not wish to

> destroy the tower, or to descend from it – rather to make it accessible to
> all. (*CE2* 169)

Woolf then turns to the new generation of writers, 'the group which began
to write about 1925 and, it may be, came to an end as a group in 1939 . . .
Day-Lewis, Auden, Spender, Isherwood, Louis MacNeice and so on' (*CE2*
170). These writers enjoy many of the same middle-class privileges as earlier
writers, but their attitude is very different:

> They are tower dwellers like their predecessors, the sons of well-to-do
> parents, who could afford to send them to public schools and
> universities. But what a difference in the tower itself, in what they saw
> from the tower! When they looked at human life what did they see?
> Everywhere change; everywhere revolution. In Germany, in Russia, in
> Italy, in Spain, all the old hedges were being rooted up; all the old towers
> were being thrown to the ground. Other hedges were being planted;
> other towers were being raised. There was communism in one country;
> in another fascism. The whole of civilization, of society, was
> changing. (*CE2* 170)

Writing in the international context of war, revolution and social upheaval,
these writers mark significant change in the production and subject matter of
literature. 'There was, it is true, neither war nor revolution in England itself.
All those writers had time to write many books before 1939. But even in
England towers that were built of gold and stucco were no longer steady
towers. They were leaning towers. The books were written under the influence of change, under the threat of war'(*CE2* 170).

Woolf examines the compromised vision of such writers, aware of their
own tower legacy, but also aware enough of life beyond to make the tower
lean. Their writing is an enabling force, one that will assist in abolishing the
tower itself: 'The leaning-tower writer has had the courage, at any rate, to
throw that little box of toys out of the window. He has had the courage to tell
the truth, the unpleasant truth, about himself' (*CE2* 177–8). She looks
forward to the 'next generation' who will be, 'when peace comes, a postwar generation too. Must it too be a leaning-tower generation – fan oblique,
sidelong, squinting, self-conscious generation with a foot in two worlds? Or
will there be no more towers and no more classes and shall we stand, without
hedges between us, on the common ground?' (*CE2* 178). This common
ground for literature, a postwar 'world without classes or towers', will be
made possible by the prospect, proffered by the politicians, of equal oppor-
tunities, equal chances of developing whatever gifts we may possess', and by
the material underpinning of that prospect by 'income tax.'

Woolf optimistically envisions that income tax will drive middle-class children from the private sector in education, 'paying twopence-halfpenny a week for that happiness and instruction instead of 35 guineas a term and extras. If the pressure of the income tax continues, classes will disappear' (*CE2* 179). She urges preparation for such a classless, postwar literary world by beginning 'now. We can begin, practically and prosaically, by borrowing books from public libraries; by reading omnivorously, simultaneously, poems, plays, novels, histories, biographies, the old and the new. We must sample before we can select . . . Of course – are we not commoners, outsiders? – we shall trample many flowers and bruise much ancient grass' (*CE2* 181). She urges us to break rules, cross class boundaries in our reading:

> Let us trespass at once. Literature is no one's private ground; literature is common ground. It is not cut up into nations; there are no wars there. Let us trespass freely and fearlessly and find our own way for ourselves. It is thus that English literature will survive this war and cross the gulf – if commoners and outsiders like ourselves make that country our own country, if we teach ourselves how to read and to write, how to preserve, and how to create.   (*CE2* 181)

Woolf's concept of the 'common ground' of literature marks out a future egalitarian, republican, democracy of letters.

In **'Thoughts on Peace in an Air Raid'** (1940), Woolf meditates, while German bombs drop on British civilian targets, on the 'queer experience, lying in the dark and listening to the zoom of a hornet which may at any moment sting you to death' (*CE4* 173). She gives warning of the gender politics inherent in this horrific aspect of modern warfare which has young men bombing unarmed women and children:

> Unless we can think peace into existence we – not this one body in its one bed but millions of bodies yet to be born – will lie in the same darkness and hear the same death rattle overhead. Let us think what we can do to create the only efficient air-raid shelter while the guns now on the hill go pop pop pop and the searchlights finger the clouds and now and then, sometimes close at hand, sometimes far away, a bomb drops.   (*CE4* 173).

The gender division of these acts has men at war with each other in the sky – 'the defenders are men, the attackers are men' – while women 'must lie weaponless to-night' listening for the bombs. But, citing William Blake's poem 'Jerusalem', Woolf urges women to 'fight with the mind', free the men 'from the machine', and 'compensate the man for the loss of his gun'

(*CE4* 174). One target is the 'subconscious Hitlerism' in men that turns them against women. In this poignant, late essay Woolf defines the 'mental fight' we should muster in times of war as fierce intellectual independence. She rallies us to think 'against the current, not with it' (*CE4* 174).

Suggested further reading

Michèle Barrett, 'Introduction' to *Virginia Woolf: Women and Writing*, ed. *Barrett* (London: Women's Press, 1979)

Rachel Bowlby, '"The Crowded Dance of Modern Life"', in Bowlby, *Feminist Destinations and Further Essays on Virginia Woolf* (Edinburgh: Edinburgh University Press, 1997)

Leila Brosnan, *Reading Virginia Woolf's Essays and Journalism* (Edinburgh: Edinburgh University Press, 1997)

Elena Gualtieri, *Virginia Woolf's Essays: Sketching the Past* (Basingstoke: Macmillan; New York: St Martin's Press, 2000)

Chapter 4

Critical reception

From the publication of her first novel in 1915, Virginia Woolf's writing received serious critical attention from reviewers and essayists. By August 1932 Woolf was complaining about 'personal appearances' and that 'my publicity is already too much for me'. Disturbed by the prospect of full-length books about her appearing, she explains:

> – not that I'm modest: not at all. But limelight is bad for me: the light in which I work best is twilight. And I'm threatened with 3 more books upon me: [Winifred] Holtby has induced another publisher to print her follies: [Dorothy] Richardson is producing another; and a man from America [Harmon H. Goldstone] a third. All this means to me a kind of fuss and falsity and talking about my husband, mother, father, and dog which I loathe.   (*L5* 97)

Today's reader of Woolf is threatened with considerably more secondary reading. Not all of the hundreds of books on Woolf that have followed in floods from this first trickle of three have talked of her 'husband, mother, father, and dog', but Woolf criticism has not altogether ignored her biographical circumstances either. As Chapter Two has discussed, biographies of Woolf do shape the critical grounds on which she is discussed. Woolf's many autobiographical writings, mostly now in print, have been enthusiastically put to work by Woolf criticism. Her letters, diaries, journals and memoirs not only provide information about her private and public life, through which some critics seek to filter her fiction, but also reveal a wealth of material about her compositional practices and writing processes. Likewise, Woolf criticism exploits her own impressive body of literary criticism. Reading criticism on Woolf is always likely to entail reading Woolf's own criticism, too.

Contemplating the threat of three more books on her, Woolf was already suspicious as well of how academic criticism would categorise her work. In November 1931 she was musing to fellow writer Hugh Walpole on how Harold Nicolson 'sweeps us all into separate schools one hostile to the other'. In a radio broadcast Nicolson had labelled Woolf as a 'modernist' along with T. S. Eliot, D. H. Lawrence, James Joyce and Evelyn Waugh, and Walpole 'old-fashioned' along with J. M. Barrie and John Galsworthy. Somewhat hypocritically, Woolf declares Nicolson 'utterly and damnably wrong, and to teach the public that's the way to read us is a crime and a scandal, and accounts for the imbecility which makes all criticism worthless' (*L4* 402). Of course, Woolf herself famously swept contemporary writers into 'separate schools' when she defined the differences between Edwardian writers (such as Arnold Bennett and Galsworthy) and Georgian writers (such as Joyce, Lawrence and Lytton Strachey), in her essays 'Modern Fiction' (1919) and 'Mr Bennett and Mrs Brown' (1924), which have been central to later academic critics' definition of modernism. But Woolf now confesses to being 'tired . . . of being caged with Aldous, Joyce and Lawrence! Can't we exchange cages for a lark? How horrified all the professors would be!' (*L4* 402). Despite her contempt for the professors, Woolf, as the author of *A Room of One's Own* (1929) and *Three Guineas* (1938), is in addition partly responsible for the cage of 'feminism' behind whose bars she also languishes in academic criticism. Her writing always straddles academic and popular realms of literature, magnificently refusing to be entirely claimed by either, but it is nevertheless responsible for the shaping of two central strands of academic critical enquiry – modernism and feminism.

Modernism and feminism are two broad axes on which Woolf criticism turns, and there are many other categories that reflect the range of positions available in literary criticism more generally, such as postmodernist, psychoanalytical, historicist, materialist, postcolonial, and so on. But before offering an account of the developments and trends in Woolf criticism from Woolf's own time to the present, it is worth pointing out to the beginning reader some points of access into Woolf studies as it currently stands.

Introductory reading

A good way to test the waters of Woolf criticism and get a sense of the cutting edge of critical debates on Woolf is to consult the *Woolf Studies Annual*, the most important international forum for serious scholarship on Woolf (by established and new scholars), established in 1995. It bears witness to the breadth and diversity of approaches to Woolf, and to continuing advances and innovations. Volume 10 (2004), for example, has two essays by eminent textual scholars on the politics of editing Woolf's work; there is an essay on Michael Cunningham's rewriting of Woolf in *The Hours*, one on ethnographic modernism in *The Voyage Out* (1915), and a whole special section of essays exploring Woolf and literary history, including an essay on Dante and *The Years* (1937), an essay on lesbian possibility in *Jacob's Room* (1922), and essays on Woolf and Borges, Woolf and Alice Munroe, and essays on reading and teaching Woolf in different contexts. The extensive review section of this issue reviews books on editing Woolf, on Woolf and science, on Woolf and the visual, on Woolf and photography, and on the European reception of Woolf, as well as books that treat Woolf in the context of modernism, of British women modernists, of the Great War, the Victorian period, and so on. Every issue of the *Woolf Studies Annual* also gives an up-to-date guide to library collections of Woolf materials, and occasionally it publishes new material that comes to light.

It is clear from browsing through the *Woolf Studies Annual* that critical debate is flourishing on every aspect of Woolf's work and life, and from every conceivable critical and theoretical position. This is also evidenced by the published proceedings of most of the Annual International Conferences on Virginia Woolf that have been held since 1990. Over the years *Modern Fiction Studies* has brought out a number of special issues on Woolf, the first in spring 1956, and the most recent in spring 2004. In this latter issue there is a range of approaches to Woolf, including essays on Woolf and Thatcherism, Woolf's shorter fiction, race, politics and aesthetics in *To the Lighthouse* (1927), Englishness in *Orlando* (1928), Woolf and Tolstoy, Woolf and ethics, and Woolf and the Great War. There is also a selected bibliography of Woolf scholarship from 1991 to 2003. The International Virginia Woolf Society publishes regularly updated bibliographies of Woolf scholarship on its web pages (http:/www.utoronto.ca/IVWS/).

As well as plunging into the *Woolf Studies Annual* and the many volumes of conference papers or special journal issues, the beginning reader might also usefully consult some of the numerous books designed to introduce Woolf's work in more orderly fashion, in the context of established areas of critical and theoretical debate. One of the most helpful is Sue Roe's and Susan Sellers's *The Cambridge Companion to Virginia Woolf* (2000), not least because each contributor (all are established Woolf scholars) gives new insights and readings in the acknowledged areas of critical focus. There are essays on Woolf and feminism, Woolf and modernism, Woolf and psychoanalysis, Woolf and Bloomsbury, Woolf and Post-Impressionism, and Woolf in socio-political context, as well as readings in Woolf's novels, essays and autobiographical writings. On the other hand, it is also useful to be guided through each of Woolf's works in turn and in the company of one commentator. Laura Marcus, for example, in *Writers and their Work: Virginia Woolf* (1997; 2nd edition, 2004), begins with discussion of Woolf's early novels, stories and essays, examining Woolf's experimentalism and her development of a new novel form, with *Jacob's Room* marking the breakthrough. Marcus then discusses Woolf's feminism in relation to *A Room of One's Own*, and her interest in representing the city in relation to *Mrs Dalloway* (1925). Woolf's later novels are then analysed in terms of their experimentalism with other genres: elegy, essay, biography and drama. Marcus opens up readings of Woolf's major works with a sensitivity to the main critical debates, and also encourages further exploration of Woolf's writing by initiating a productive process of attentive close reading.

Beginning readers also need guidance through the various critical approaches that have developed over the decades since Woolf's death. John Mepham's *Criticism in Focus: Virginia Woolf* (1992) offers a manageable and brief overview of Woolf criticism, organising it in terms of biography, context, modernism, feminism, philosophy, practical criticism, and editions and drafts. Mepham does no more than usefully summarise in outline the enormous range of critical material he covers. His commentary is useful in conjunction with the many collections that bring together key sample essays and extracts from the best and most influential of Woolf criticism, such as Rachel Bowlby's critical reader, *Virginia Woolf* (1992), and my *The Icon Critical Guide to Virginia Woolf* (1997). Anna Snaith has edited a useful collection of essays specially commissioned from Woolf scholars invited to take stock of the main trends in Woolf criticism. Her *Palgrave Advances in Virginia Woolf Studies* (2006) includes chapters on feminist approaches, narratological approaches, biographical approaches, psychoanalytical approaches, modernist approaches, historicist approaches, postmodern and poststructuralist approaches, bibliographical approaches, lesbian approaches, postcolonial approaches, and European reception studies. Mark Hussey's *Virginia Woolf A to Z* (1995) provides thorough accounts of all Woolf's works with information on their genesis and critical reception.

Critical reception

Woolf criticism has not evolved smoothly, and it would be misleading to say that any one approach or interpretation has ever prevailed to the exclusion of others. There are continuities and discontinuities in trends and arguments, areas of common ground and major points of dispute. In what follows, developments in Woolf studies are discussed chronologically, but the chronological demarcation of many trends is by no means strict. This survey of the criticism also connects with discussions of Woolf's works and their reception in Chapter Three and with the outline of the broader movements of cultural reception and biographical slant charted in Chapter Two. It would be impossible, within the confines of this chapter, as well as confusing, to cover in detail the entirety of Woolf criticism. For the purposes of clarity and economy, each subsection gives an account of one or two critics as exemplary of wider approaches, or where a critic has given a new direction to readings in Woolf.

Contemporary reviews and the 1940s: innovation, experimentalism, impressionism

I have given some indication, in Chapter Three, of some of her contemporaries' private and public responses to Woolf's major works, drawing on the standard source of the first published critical reception of her writing, Robin Majumdar's and Allen McLaurin's *Virginia Woolf: The Critical Heritage* (1975). As this body of reviews and essays shows, Woolf's work was received with serious critical interest from her first publication. She was greeted as an innovator of experimental form, 'impressionism' and stream-of-consciousness and held up for comparison with contemporaries such as James Joyce, Marcel Proust and Dorothy Richardson. As we have seen in Chapter Three, her neglect of plot and character prompted dismay in some reviewers such as her critical sparring partner, Arnold Bennett; and Katherine Mansfield's review of her second novel, *Night and Day* (1919), seems to have stung Woolf deeply.

In the 1930s, as Woolf's reputation grew, and in the 1940s in the aftermath of her death, a number of book-length studies of her work appeared. This was a period when critics sought to encapsulate Woolf's achievements and qualities, to sum up her enormous contribution to modern literature. As well as glowing recognition of a significant modern talent in some quarters, there also came doubt, reservation and hostility from others. Floris Delattre's

Le Roman Psychologique de Virginia Woolf (1932) draws on Henri Bergson's philosophy to discuss the subjective and the temporal in Woolf's writing, and anticipates a dominant strand of Bergsonian interpretations of Woolf. The novelist Winifred Holtby's book, *Virginia Woolf: A Critical Memoir* (1932) is one of the earliest to discuss Woolf's feminist politics. Ruth Gruber, the youngest person in the world at that time to be awarded a Ph.D., published her dissertation, *Virginia Woolf: A Study*, in 1935. This incisive work offers a thoroughgoing analysis of the polarities of Woolf's feminist aesthetics and of her densely allusive writing, tracing her intellectual influences and her engagement with numerous contemporary and historical literary and philosophical texts. Gruber is particularly penetrating on the feminist politics of Woolf's avant-garde style in *Orlando* and *A Room of One's Own*, and offers illuminating readings of Woolf's other major essays and novels up to and including *The Waves*.[1]

David Daiches's excellent *Virginia Woolf* (1942) offers sensitive readings of her symbolism and aesthetic technique. As early as 1931, William Empson hailed Woolf as a writer of Shakespeare's stature, praising her symbolism, her impressionism, and her 'glittering and searching' imagery (*CH* 308). Wyndham Lewis, on the other hand, satirised Woolf and Bloomsbury aesthetics savagely in *Men Without Art* (1934), deriding her feminism and her 'feminine principle' (*CH* 331). Q. D. Leavis inflicted some lasting wounds to Woolf's reputation in her class-based attack on the deplorable 'sex-hostility' of *Three Guineas* (*CH* 419), later compounded by F. R. Leavis's indictment of Woolf's 'sophisticated aestheticism' for its 'lack of moral interest and interest in action'.[2] E. M. Forster paid mixed tribute to Woolf in his Rede Lecture for Cambridge University in 1941, acknowledging her triumph as an artist but also pointing up what he considered her flaws – poeticism and feminism. John Hawley Roberts, in his article "Vision and Design' in Virginia Woolf" (1946), was one of the first critics to read Woolf through the formalist theories of her Bloomsbury colleague Roger Fry.

The most important and influential work on Woolf in this period, however, is Erich Auerbach's chapter on *To the Lighthouse* in his landmark book, *Mimesis: The Representation of Reality in Western Literature* (1946). Here Auerbach closes his survey of Western literature from Homer to the present with a detailed analysis of a passage from Woolf's novel, which he examines in terms of point of view, narrative voice, time, interior and exterior consciousness, epistemology and fragmentation. He identifies her modern literary technique as a new model for the organisation of thought and language, his own philological template, in fact. Like Empson, he acknowledges Woolf's achievement as a major European writer, already attaining the status of classic.

The 1950s and 1960s: philosophy, psychology, myth

There was considerable critical interest in Woolf's life and work in this period, fuelled by the publication of selected extracts from her diaries, in *A Writer's Diary* (1953), and in part by J. K. Johnstone's *The Bloomsbury Group* (1954). The main critical impetus was to establish a sense of a unifying aesthetic mode in Woolf's writing, and in her works as a whole, whether through philosophy, psychoanalysis, formal aesthetics, or mythopoeisis. James Hafley identified a cosmic philosophy in his detailed analysis of her fiction, *The Glass Roof: Virginia Woolf as Novelist* (1954), and offered a complex account of her symbolism. Woolf featured in the influential *The English Novel: A Short Critical History* (1954) by Walter Allen who, with antique chauvinism, describes the Woolfian 'moment' in terms of 'short, sharp female gasps of ecstasy, an impression intensified by Mrs Woolf's use of the semi-colon where the comma is ordinarily enough'.[3] Psychological and Freudian interpretations were also emerging at this time, such as Joseph Blotner's 1956 study of mythic patterns in *To the Lighthouse*, an essay that draws on Freud, Jung and the myth of Persephone.[4] And there were studies of Bergsonian writing that made much of Woolf, such as Shiv Kumar's *Bergson and the Stream of Consciousness Novel* (1962).

The most important work of this period was by the French critic Jean Guiguet. His *Virginia Woolf and Her Works* (1962; translated by Jean Stewart, 1965) was the first full-length study of Woolf's oeuvre, and it stood for a long time as the standard work of critical reference in Woolf studies. Guiguet draws on the existentialism of Jean-Paul Sartre to put forward a philosophical reading of Woolf; and he also introduces a psychobiographical dimension in his heavy use of extracts from *A Writer's Diary*. He lays great emphasis on subjectivism in Woolf's writing, and draws attention to her interest in the subjective experience of 'the moment.' Despite his philosophical apparatus, Guiguet refuses to categorise Woolf in terms of any one school, and insists that Woolf has indeed 'no pretensions to abstract thought: her domain is life, not ideology'. Her avoidance of conventional character makes Woolf for him a 'purely psychological' writer.[5] Guiguet set a trend against materialist and historicist readings of Woolf by his insistence on the primacy of the subjective and the psychological: 'To exist, for Virginia Woolf, meant experiencing that dizziness on the ridge between two abysses of the unknown, the self and the non-self.'[6] This existentialist approach did not foreground Woolf's feminism, either.

The 1970s and 1980s: feminism, androgyny, modernism, aesthetics

In the 1970s and 1980s, Woolf studies expanded in a number of directions, most notably in relation to feminism. Critical interest in Woolf developed at the same time as feminism developed in related academic disciplines. In this period her writings became central to the theoretical framing of feminism, in particular to debates on Marxist and materialist feminism and to the emergent theories of androgyny. Both these areas of debate take Woolf's *A Room of One's Own* as a major point of reference. As I discussed in Chapter Three, it is in this text that Woolf puts forward a materialist argument about the production of women's literature and outlines her theory of androgynous writing, which she developed from Samuel Taylor Coleridge.

At the same time as feminist approaches to Woolf were developing and expanding, so, too, was the critical interest in her modernist theories and her formal aesthetics. Again, Woolf's writing became central to critical and theoretical formulations on modernism. As we have seen in Chapter Three, her essays 'Modern Fiction' and 'Mr Bennett and Mrs Brown' became critical touchstones for modernist criticism, and Woolf's fiction became the object of sustained formalist scrutiny, especially in relation to Bloomsbury's formalist theories of the visual arts as propounded by Clive Bell and Roger Fry. In this period critical approaches tended to diverge between modernist (or formalist) and feminist readings. But both tendencies evinced a marked move away from the earlier critical impulses to uncover a unifying vision in Woolf's work, recognising instead a dualism or oppositional force in her writing. There were also many points of critical friction between those interpreting Woolf as an aesthete and those who followed her feminism.

Following on from Carolyn Heilbrun's landmark work on androgyny, *Towards Androgyny: Aspects of Male and Female in Literature* (1963), two books appeared in 1973 on Woolf and androgyny by Alice Van Buren Kelley and Nancy Topping Bazin. Woolf's theory of androgyny has been understood as both synthesising and perpetuating gender difference. Kelley and Bazin found a mystical synthesis at work in Woolf's theory, which Elaine Showalter attacked as unfeminist in her influential critique of Woolf in 'Virginia Woolf and the Flight into Androgyny', a chapter in her 1977 book *A Literature of Their Own: British Women Novelists from Brontë to Lessing*. Showalter expresses puzzlement at Woolf's experimental narrative form in *A Room of One's Own*, concluding that it deflects from her feminist argument.

Marxist and materialist feminism, on the other hand, found its own confirmation in Woolf's writing, particularly as presented in Michèle Barrett's important and influential collection of Woolf's feminist essays, *Virginia Woolf on Women and Writing* (1979). Jane Marcus, whose feminist criticism of Woolf came to dominate in the 1980s, consolidated materialist-feminist readings of Woolf in her monographs, *Art and Anger: Reading Like a Woman* (1988) and *Virginia Woolf and the Languages of Patriarchy* (1988), and established the breadth and range of feminist interpretations of Woolf in her edited collections, *New Feminist Essays on Virginia Woolf* (1981), *Virginia Woolf: A Feminist Slant* (1983) and *Virginia Woolf and Bloomsbury: A Centenary Celebration* (1987). Along with Madeline Moore, in her *The Short Season Between Two Silences: The Mystical and the Political in the Novels of Virginia Woolf* (1984), and many others, Marcus politicised aspects of Woolf's writing (such as her perceived 'mysticism') that had previously been understood as 'apolitical', at the same time as acknowledging the significance of Woolf's work for feminism. Alex Zwerdling's book *Virginia Woolf and the Real World* (1986) was influential, too, in locating Woolf's writing in historical and political context.

Formalist and modernist criticism on Woolf was also rapidly developing in the 1970s and 1980s. Malcolm Bradbury and James McFarlane, in *Modernism 1890–1930* (1976), Peter Faulkner's reader, *Modernism* (1977), and David Lodge, in his various readers and exegeses of modern criticism, confirmed Woolf as a key authority for modernist aesthetics. Significant essays by critics such as Geoffrey Hartman and J. W. Graham explored the formal complexities of Woolf's writing and compositional processes. Hartman, in 'Virginia's Web' (1970), examined aesthetic order and disorder in *To the Lighthouse* and *Mrs Dalloway*, anticipating later deconstructionist approaches to Woolf.[7] In this period when holograph and draft editions of Woolf's major works were beginning to appear, Graham, in 'Point of View in *The Waves*', conducted a pioneering analysis of Woolf's drafts to explore her narratological development.[8] Mitchell Leaska put forward an intensive and rigorous formalist analysis in his book-length study, *Virginia Woolf's Lighthouse: A Study in Critical Method* (1970). Hermione Lee perpetuated a more readable close-reading approach to Woolf in her monograph, *The Novels of Virginia Woolf* (1977).

This period also saw considerable critical interest in the influence of the visual arts on Woolf's writing, and particularly in the influence of the formalist theories of her Bloomsbury colleagues Roger Fry and Clive Bell.

Jack F. Stewart, for example, published a series of important essays on light, form and colour in Woolf's writing;[9] and Allen McLaurin, in *Virginia Woolf: The Echoes Enslaved* (1973), examined Woolf's work in the light of the aesthetic theories of Roger Fry and G. E. Moore. Maria Torgovnick connects Woolf's writing with Fry's formalism in *The Visual Arts, Pictorialism and the Novel: James, Lawrence and Woolf* (1985); and Diane Gillespie's landmark book, *The Sisters' Arts: The Writing and Painting of Virginia Woolf and Vanessa Bell* (1988), establishes the central importance of Woolf's sister, the artist Vanessa Bell, as a professional influence on Woolf. Gillespie encourages readers to look beyond the theories of Fry and Clive Bell, to consider the material practice of Vanessa Bell, and to take more seriously her collaboration with Woolf in many of her works.

Gillian Beer, on the other hand, explored the philosophical legacy of Woolf's father, Leslie Stephen, in her influential essay 'Hume, Stephen and Elegy in *To the Lighthouse*' (1984). Beer's work on Woolf's intellectual origins has been enormously influential. Her interest in Woolf's engagement with the genre of elegy and with mourning in general has been picked up by a number of Woolf critics. Her book *Arguing with the Past: Essays in Narrative from Woolf to Sidney* (1989) contains four important essays on Woolf. These and further essays have been collected in Beer's *Virginia Woolf: The Common Ground* (1996). Perry Meisel, in *The Absent Father: Virginia Woolf and Walter Pater* (1980), departs from the critical trend of exploring well-documented influences on Woolf, to consider Woolf's largely unacknowledged debt to her predecessor in literary aesthetics, Walter Pater. This is a fascinating book, not only for the case it makes for Paterian readings in Woolf, but also for its sophisticated opening up of Woolf's writing to the possibilities of deconstructive readings.

The 1980s: feminism, postmodernism, sexual/textual politics

While it might be tempting to generalise that Woolf's writing was being discussed almost in two separate camps during the 1980s, formalists on the one hand, and feminists on the other, this would be to simplify things too far. Many critics were attempting to make sense of and connect her feminist politics with her modernist practices. Such investigations coincided with the explosion of theory in literary studies, and once again the work of Virginia Woolf was central to the framing of many of the major theoretical developments in literary critical engagements with feminism, postmodernism, deconstruction and psychoanalysis. In the context of the rise of 'high theory' and the questioning of old-school Marxist, materialist, humanist and historicist literary theories, Woolf studies wrestled with the locating of her radical feminist politics in the avant-garde qualities of the text itself, and its endlessly transgressive play of signifiers, with the Woolfian inscription of radically deconstructed models of the self and of sexuality and *jouissance.*

Woolf's writing, furthermore, was often the territory over which feminism's struggles with postmodernism were conducted in this period. Indeed, one of the most influential works of literary criticism to emerge in the 1980s was Toril Moi's indispensable introduction to French feminist theory, *Sexual/ Textual Politics: Feminist Literary Theory* (1985), in which Woolf's writing is the main focus of argument. Moi begins by considering the debates over Woolf's feminism that emerged in the 1970s. She argues with Elaine Showalter's critique of Woolf's theory of androgyny, and claims androgyny and textual experimentalism as the basis for understanding Woolf's radical sexual, textual politics. In her introductory sections, 'Who's Afraid of Virginia Woolf? Feminist Readings of Woolf', and 'Rescuing Woolf for Feminist Politics: Some Points Toward an Alternative Reading', Moi recommends the new French feminist theories of Julia Kristeva, Hélène Cixous, and Luce Irigaray as the most pertinent for reading Woolf's fiction and nonfiction. She invokes the deconstructive theories of Jacques Derrida and the post-Freudian, psychoanalytical theories of Jacques Lacan, to enforce her case. As well as denouncing Showalter as an unwitting Marxist humanist, Moi criticises the materialist feminism of Barrett, Marcus, and Kate Millett (the premises of whose famous book, *Sexual Politics,* Moi implicitly overturns). Although she acknowledges Beer as an influence, as well as Meisel's early deconstructionist reading of Woolf, Moi seems unaware, in *Sexual/ Textual Politics,* of Gayatri Chakravorti Spivak's groundbreaking feminist-deconstructionist reading of Woolf in her essay 'Unmaking and Making in *To the Lighthouse*' (1980).[10]

Makiko Minow-Pinkney's *Virginia Woolf and the Problem of the Subject* (1987) was one of the first book-length studies of Woolf's work to implement French feminist theory. It remains essential reading. Also essential is Rachel Bowlby's landmark book, *Virginia Woolf: Feminist Destinations* (1988), which puts forward a psychoanalytical reading of Woolf's feminism, making the case for more open, multiple and shifting readings. This book is central to both Woolf studies and feminist studies more generally. A new edition, with a further five essays on Woolf, was published as *Feminist Destinations and Further Essays on Virginia Woolf* in 1997. Woolf was clearly central in postmodernist critical engagements with modernism.

The 1990s to the present: feminism, historicism, postcolonialism, ethics

There has never been a better time to study Virginia Woolf. Woolf studies, in the 1990s and in the new millennium, has continued to flourish and diversify in all its numerous and proliferating aspects. In this recent period the topics that occupied earlier critics continue in new debates, on her modernism, her philosophy and ethics, her feminism and her aesthetics; and there have also been marked turns in new directions. Woolf and her work have been increasingly examined in the context of empire, drawing on the influential field of postcolonial studies; and, stimulated by the impetus of new historicism and cultural materialism, there have been new attempts to understand Woolf's writing and persona in the context of the public and private spheres, in the present as well as in her own time. Woolf in the context of war and fascism, and in the contexts of modernity, science and technology, continue to exercise critics. Serious, sustained readings of lesbianism in Woolf's writing and in her life have marked recent feminist interpretations in Woolf studies. Enormous advances have also been made in the study of Woolf's literary and cultural influences and allusions. Numerous annotated and scholarly editions of Woolf's works have been appearing since she briefly came out of copyright in 1991, accompanied by several more scholarly editions of her works in draft and holograph, encouraging further critical scrutiny of her compositional methods. There have been several important reference works on Woolf. Many biographies of Woolf and her circle have also appeared, renewing biographical criticism, along with a number of works concerned with Woolf in geographical context, from landscape and London sites to Woolf's and her circle's many houses and holiday retreats.

Jane Marcus's widely disseminated essay, 'Britannia Rules *The Waves*' (1992), along with Kathy J. Phillips's book, *Virginia Woolf Against Empire* (1994), established Woolf's engagement with empire and race as a central critical concern in Woolf studies. Anna Snaith's topic for the 2005 Virginia Woolf Society of Great Britain's Annual Virginia Woolf Birthday Lecture was 'Virginia Woolf and Empire'. Marcus's essay has been reprinted recently in her book *Hearts of Darkness: White Women Write Race* (2004), which also includes a thoroughgoing examination of the controversial 'fine negress' passage in *A Room of One's Own*, discussed in Chapter Three. This continues to be a keenly debated area of Woolf studies.

Eileen Barrett's and Patricia Cramer's collection, *Virginia Woolf: Lesbian Readings* (1997) is a key work for lesbian studies in Woolf, and lesbian and queer criticism of Woolf continues to flourish. Mark Hussey's collection of essays by various Woolf scholars, *Virginia Woolf and War: Fiction, Reality and Myth* (1991), and Karen L. Levenback's *Virginia Woolf and the Great War* (1999) are two of several works on Woolf and war. Merry Pawlowski edited a collection of essays on Woolf and fascism (2001). Woolf in social, historical and political context has been addressed by a number of critics, including David Bradshaw, in his key essays for the *Woolf Studies Annual*;[11] Jessica Berman, in *Modernist Fiction, Cosmopolitanism, and the Politics of Community* (2001); Anna Snaith, in her influential book *Virginia Woolf: Public and Private Negotiations* (2000); and Linden Peach's helpful contextual reading of Woolf, *Virginia Woolf: Critical Issues* (2000).

Woolf's essays have been the object of considerable critical attention in this period, notably by Leila Brosnan, in *Reading Virginia Woolf's Essays and Journalism: Breaking the Surface of Silence* (1997), and Elena Gualtieri, in *Virginia Woolf's Essays: Sketching the Past* (2000), as well as by Beth Carole Rosenberg's and Jeanne Dubino's collection, *Virginia Woolf and the Essay* (1997). These works have looked at Woolf's engagement with other writers, past and contemporary, and have enhanced developments in the research of Woolf's literary and cultural influences. The *Woolf Studies Annual* has published two issues of articles on Woolf and literary history (volumes 9 and 10), and there have been a number of important books in the field, such as Ellen Tremper's '*Who Lived at Alfoxton?': Virginia Woolf and English Romanticism* (1998) and Juliet Dusinberre's book on Elizabethan influences on Woolf, *Virginia Woolf's Renaissance: Woman Reader or Common Reader?* (1997).

There have also been significant publications on Woolf and modernity, science and technology in these years, including Pamela Caughie's edited collection *Virginia Woolf in the Age of Mechanical Reproduction* (2000), Michael Whitworth's *Einstein's Wake: Relativity, Metaphor, and Modernist Literature* (2001) and Holly Henry's *Virginia Woolf and the Discourse of Science* (2003). Woolf's position regarding class remains elusive and unsettled in the minds of critics, and continues to raise controversy, as suggested by the bumpy reception of, Sonya Rudikoff's *Ancestral Houses: Virginia Woolf and the Aristocracy* (1999).[12] The geographical contexts of Woolf's life and works are of current critical interest, too. For example, Katherine C. Hill-Miller combines literary criticism with the most detailed guide so far to the physical geographies of both life and works in *From the Lighthouse to Monk's House: A Guide to Virginia Woolf's Literary Landscapes* (2001).

Nevertheless, Woolf's place in the frames of modernism and feminism remains the dominant concern of Woolf studies, as exemplified in three recent books: Ann Banfield's detailed and erudite work on the philosophical influences on Woolf's modernism, *The Phantom Table: Woolf, Fry, Russell and the Epistemology of Modernism* (2000), Maggie Humm's important feminist reading of Woolf's visual modernism, *Modernist Women and Visual Cultures: Virginia Woolf, Vanessa Bell, Photography and Cinema* (2003), and Naomi Black's timely return to Woolf's feminism, *Virginia Woolf as Feminist* (2004). In *Virginia Woolf and the Bloomsbury Avant-Garde: War, Civilisation and Modernity* (2005), Christine Froula offers illuminating readings of Woolf's novels in the intellectual context of modernist aesthetics and radical Enlightenment Philosophies. She demonstrates Woolf's continuing central significance for modern thought, modern politics and modern writing.

Notes

1 Life

1. Susan Sellers, 'Virginia Woolf's Diaries and Letters', in Sue Roe and Susan Sellers (eds.), *The Cambridge Companion to Virginia Woolf*, (Cambridge: Cambridge University Press, 2000), p. 109.
2. See Virginia Woolf and Vanessa Bell, with Thoby Stephen, *The Hyde Park Gate News: The Stephen Family Newspaper*, ed. Gill Lowe (London: Hesperus, 2005).
3. Virginia Woolf. *A Passionate Apprentice: The Early Journals 1897–1909*, ed. Mitchell A. Leaska (London: Hogarth, 1990), p. 42.
4. Leonard Woolf, *Beginning Again: An Autobiography of the Years 1911 to 1918* (London: Hogarth, 1965), p. 24.
5. Vanessa Bell, 'Notes on Bloomsbury' (1951), in *Sketches in Pen and Ink: A Bloomsbury Notebook*, ed. Lia Giachero (London: Chatto & Windus, 1998), p. 105.
6. Vanessa Bell, 'Life at Hyde Park Gate after 1897' (n.d.), in *Sketches in Pen and Ink*, p. 81.
7. Violet Dickinson's copy of 'Friendships Gallery' is now in the Berg Collection, New York Public Library. See Ellen Hawkes's edition in *Twentieth Century Literature* 25.3/4 (Autumn/Winter 1979), pp. 270–302.
8. See Sarah M. Hall, *Before Leonard: The Early Suitors of Virginia Woolf* (London: Peter Owen, 2000).
9. Frances Spalding, *Roger Fry: Art and Life* (London: Elek, 1980), p. 139.
10. Woolf, *Beginning Again*, pp. 26–7, 35.
11. Vita Sackville-West to Harold Nicolson, 17 August 1926; quoted in Suzanne Raitt, *Vita & Virginia: the Work and Friendship of Vita Sackville-West and Virginia Woolf* (Oxford: Oxford University Press, 1993), p. 2.
12. Raitt, *Vita & Virginia*, p.2.
13. Ibid., pp. 3–4.
14. David Bradshaw, 'British Writers and Anti-Fascism in the 1930s, Part I: The Bray and Drone of Tortured Voices', *Woolf Studies Annual* 3 (1997), pp. 3–27, and 'British Writers and Anti-Fascism in the 1930s, Part II: Under the Hawk's Wings', *Woolf Studies Annual* 4 (1998), pp. 41–66.
15. Bradshaw, 'British Writers and Anti-Fascism in the 1930s, Part I', p. 22.

16. Bradshaw, 'British Writers and Anti-Fascism in the 1930s, Part II', p. 48.
17. Ibid.

2 Contexts

1. Leonard Woolf, *Downhill All the Way: An Autobiography of the Years 1919–1939* (London: Hogarth, 1967), p. 27.
2. Clive Bell, *Old Friends: Personal Recollections* (London: Chatto & Windus 1956), p. 101.
3. Quentin Bell, *Guardian* (21 March 1982), quoted in Jane Marcus 'Quentin's Bogey', *Critical Inquiry* 11 (1985), p. 492.
4. Brenda Silver, *Virginia Woolf Icon* (Chicago: University of Chicago Press, 1999), p. xvii.
5. Ibid., p. 11.

3 Works

1. Virginia Woolf, '*Flumina Amen Silvasque*' (1917), *E2* 161–5. See William Blake, *Milton A Poem: And the Final Illuminated Works*, ed. Robest N. Essick and Joseph Viscomi (London: The William Blake Trust/Tate Gallery, 1993).
2. George Gordon, Lord Byron, *Don Juan*, ed. T. G. Steffan, E. Steffan and W. W. Pratt with revisions by T. G. Steffan (Harmondsworth: Penguin, 1977).
3. *Virginia Woolf and Lytton Strachey: Letters*, ed. Leonard Woolf and James Strachey (London: Hogarth, 1956), p. 73.

4 Critical reception

1. Ruth Gruber, who received her doctorate from Cologne University in 1931 at the age of twenty, has published a new edition of this work as *Virginia Woolf: The Will to Create as a Woman* (New York: Caroll & Graf, 2005).
2. F. R. Leavis, 'After *To the Lighthouse*', *Scrutiny* 10 (January 1942), pp. 295–8.
3. Walter Allen, *The English Novel: A Short Critical History* (London: Phoenix House, 1954), p. 335.
4. Joseph L. Blotner, 'Mythic Patterns in *To the Lighthouse*', *PMLA* 71 (1956), pp. 547–62.
5. Jean Guiguet, *Virginia Woolf and Her Works* (1962), trans. Jean Stewart (London: Hogarth, 1965), pp. 460, 253.
6. Ibid., p. 461.

7. Geoffrey Hartman, 'Virginia's Web', in Hartman, *Beyond Formalism: Literary Essays 1958–1970* (New Haven: Yale University Press, 1970).

8. J. W. Graham, 'Point of View in *The Waves*: Some Services of Style', *University of Toronto Quarterly* 39 (1969–70), pp. 193–211.

9. Jack F. Stewart, 'Existence and Symbol in *The Waves*', *Modern Fiction Studies* 18.3 (Autumn 1972), pp. 433–7; 'Light in *To the Lighthouse*', *Twentieth Century Literature* 23 (1977), pp. 377–89; 'Form and Color in *The Waves*', *Twentieth Century Literature* 28 (1982), pp. 86–101; and 'Color in *To the Lighthouse*', *Twentieth Century Literature* 31 (1985), pp. 438–58.

10. Gayatri Chakravorti Spivak, 'Unmaking and Making in *To the Lighthouse*' (1980), in Spivak, *Other Worlds: Essays in Cultural Politics* (London: Methuen, 1987).

11. David Bradshaw, 'British Writers and Anti-Fascism in the 1930s, Part I: The Bray and Drone of Tortured Voices', *Woolf Studies Annual* 3 (1997), pp. 3–27; 'British Writers and Anti-Fascism in the 1930s, Part II: Under the Hawk's Wings', *Woolf Studies Annual* 4 (1998), pp. 41–66; and ' "Vanished, Like Leaves": The Military, Elegy and Italy in *Mrs Dalloway*', *Woolf Studies Annual* 8 (1998), pp. 107–25.

12. See Melba Cuddy-Keane, '*Ancestral Houses: Virginia Woolf and the Aristocracy* (review)', *Modern Fiction Studies* 48.2 (Summer 2002), pp. 526–8.

Guide to further reading

Virginia Woolf's works

Novels

The Voyage Out (London: Duckworth, 1915)
Night and Day (London: Duckworth, 1919)
Jacob's Room (London: Hogarth, 1922)
Mrs Dalloway (London: Hogarth, 1925)
To the Lighthouse (London: Hogarth, 1927)
Orlando: A Biography (London: Hogarth, 1928)
The Waves (London: Hogarth, 1931)
Flush: A Biography (London: Hogarth, 1933)
The Years (London: Hogarth, 1937)
Between the Acts (London: Hogarth, 1941)

Short stories

The Complete Shorter Fiction of Virginia Woolf, ed. Susan Dick, 2nd edn (London: Hogarth, 1989)

Drama

Freshwater: A Comedy, ed. Lucio Ruotolo (London: Hogarth, 1976)

Non-fiction

A Room of One's Own (London: Hogarth, 1929)
Three Guineas (London: Hogarth, 1938)
Roger Fry: A Biography (London: Hogarth, 1940)

Essays

The Common Reader (London: Hogarth, 1925)
The Common Reader: Second Series (London: Hogarth, 1932)
The Moment and Other Essays (London: Hogarth, 1947)
Collected Essays, 4 vols., ed. Leonard Woolf (London: Hogarth, 1966–7)
Virginia Woolf: Women and Writing, ed. Michèle Barrett (London: Women's Press, 1979)
The Essays of Virginia Woolf, vols. 1–4 (of 6), ed. Andrew McNeillie (London: Hogarth, 1986–94)
Moments of Being, ed. Jeanne Schulkind, 2nd edn (London: Hogarth, 1985)
The London Scene (London: Snowbooks, 2004)

Diaries, journals, letters

The Letters of Virginia Woolf (1888–1941), 6 vols., ed. Nigel Nicolson and Joanne Trautman (London: Hogarth, 1975–80)
The Diary of Virginia Woolf (1915–1941), 5 vols., ed. Anne Olivier Bell and Andrew McNeillie (London: Hogarth, 1977–84)
Virginia Woolf's Reading Notebooks, ed. Brenda Silver (Princeton: Princeton University Press, 1983)
A Passionate Apprentice: The Early Journals 1897–1909, ed. Mitchell A. Leaska (London: Hogarth, 1990)

Holograph and draft editions

The Pargiters: The Novel-Essay Portion of 'The Years', ed. Mitchell A. Leaska (London: Hogarth, 1978)
Pointz Hall: The Earlier and Later Typescripts of 'Between the Acts', ed. Mitchell A. Leaska (New York: J. Jay Press, 1982)
To the Lighthouse: The Original Holograph Draft, ed. Susan Dick (Toronto and London: University of Toronto Press, 1983)
The Waves: The Two Holograph Drafts, ed. J. W. Graham (London: Hogarth, 1983)
Women & Fiction: The Manuscript Versions of 'A Room of One's Own', ed. S. P. Rosenbaum (Oxford: Shakespeare Head, Blackwell, 1992)
Orlando: The Holograph Draft, ed. Stuart N. Clarke (London: S. N. Clarke, 1993)
Virginia Woolf's 'The Hours': The British Museum Manuscript of 'Mrs Dalloway', ed. Helen M. Wussow (New York: Pace University Press, 1996)
Virginia Woolf's 'Jacob's Room': The Holograph Draft, ed. Edward Bishop (New York: Pace University Press, 1998)

Melymbrosia: An Early Version of 'The Voyage Out', ed. Louise DeSalvo (San
      Francisco: Cleis Press, 2002)

Secondary Sources

Selected biographies

Bell, Quentin, *Virginia Woolf: A Biography,* 2 vols. (London: Hogarth, 1972)
Briggs, Julia, *Virginia Woolf: An Inner Life* (London: Penguin, 2005)
Fuegi, John, and Jo Francis (dirs.), *The War Within: A Portrait of Virginia Woolf*
      DVD (Flare Films: 1995)
Gordon, Lyndall, *Virginia Woolf: A Writer's Life* (Oxford: Oxford University
      Press, 1984)
Lee, Hermione, *Virginia Woolf* (London: Chatto & Windus, 1996)
Reid, Panthea, *Art and Affection: A Life of Virginia Woolf* (New York: Oxford
      University Press, 1996)

Selected journals

Woolf Studies Annual (1995–)
Virginia Woolf Bulletin (1999–)
Modern Fiction Studies Special Issues on Virginia Woolf: Spring 1956; Autumn
      1972; Spring 1992; Spring 2004
South Carolina Review Special Issue on Virginia Woolf: Autumn 1996
Women's Studies: An Interdisciplinary Journal Special Issue: 'Virginia Woolf in
      Performance' (August 1999) ed. Sally Greene

Bibliography

Kirkpatrick, B. J., and Stuart N. Clarke, *A Bibliography of Virginia Woolf,* 4th edn
      (Oxford and New York: Clarendon, 1997)

Selected recommended criticism and reference works

Barrett, Eileen, and Patricia Cramer (eds.) *Virginia Woolf: Lesbian Readings* (New
      York: New York University Press, 1997)
Beer, Gillian, *Virginia Woolf: The Common Ground* (Edinburgh: Edinburgh
      University Press, 1996)
Black, Naomi, *Virginia Woolf as Feminist* (Ithaca, NY: Cornell University Press,
      2004)

Bowlby, Rachel, *Feminist Destinations and Further Essays on Virginia Woolf* (Edinburgh: Edinburgh University Press, 1997)

(ed.), *Virginia Woolf* (London: Longman, 1992)

Caws, Mary Ann, and Nicola Luckhurst (eds.), *The Reception of Virginia Woolf in Europe* (London: Continuum, 2002)

Chapman, Wayne, and Janet Manson (eds.), *Women in the Milieu of Leonard and Virginia Woolf: Peace, Politics, and Education* (New York: Pace University Press, 1998)

Froula, Christine *Virginia Woolf and the Bloomsbury Avant-Garde: War, Civilisation and Modernity* (New York: Columbia University Press, 2005)

Goldman, Jane, (ed.), *The Icon Critical Guide to Virginia Woolf* (Cambridge: Icon, 1997)

Greene, Sally (ed.), *Virginia Woolf: Reading the Renaissance* (Athens, OH: Ohio University Press, 1999)

Gruber, Ruth, *Virginia Woolf: The Will to Create as a Woman* (New York: Carroll & Graf, 2005)

Gualtieri, Eleanor, *Virginia Woolf's Essays: Sketching the Past* (Basingstoke: Macmillan, 2000)

Homans, Margaret (ed.), *Virginia Woolf: A Collection of Critical Essays* (Englewood Cliffs, NJ: Prentice Hall, 1993)

Hussey, Mark, *Virginia Woolf A to Z: A Comprehensive Reference for Students, Teachers, and Common Readers to Her Life, Work and Critical Reception* (New York: Facts on File, 1995)

(ed.), *Virginia Woolf and War: Fiction, Reality and Myth* (Syracuse: Syracuse University Press, 1991)

McNees, Eleanor (ed.), *Virginia Woolf: Critical Assessments*, 4 vols. (New York: Helm Information, 1994)

Majumdar, Robin, and Allen McLaurin (eds.), *Virginia Woolf: The Critical Heritage* (London: Routledge, 1975)

Marcus, Jane, *Hearts of Darkness: White Women Write Race* (New Brunswick, NJ: Rutgers University Press, 2004)

(ed.), *New Feminist Essays on Virginia Woolf* (Lincoln and London: University of Nebraska Press, 1981)

(ed.), *Virginia Woolf: A Feminist Slant* (Lincoln: University of Nebraska Press, 1983)

Marcus, Laura, *Writers and Their Work: Virginia Woolf*, 2nd edn (Plymouth: Northcote House, 2004)

Mepham, John, *Criticism in Focus: Virginia Woolf* (London: Bristol Classical Press, 1992)

Merli, Carol (ed.), *Illuminations: New Readings of Virginia Woolf* (New Delhi: Macmillan, 2004)

Oldfield, Sybil (ed.), *Afterwords: Letters on the Death of Virginia Woolf* (Edinburgh: Edinburgh University Press, 2005)

Peach, Linden, *Virginia Woolf* (Basingstoke: Macmillan, 2000)

Pawlowski, Merry (ed.), *Virginia Woolf and Fascism: Resisting the Dictators' Seduction* (New York: Palgrave, 2001)

Raitt, Suzanne, *Vita & Virginia: The Work and Friendship of Vita Sackville-West and Virginia Woolf* (Oxford: Oxford University Press, 1993)

Roe, Sue, and Susan Sellers (eds.), *The Cambridge Companion to Virginia Woolf* (Cambridge: Cambridge University Press, 2000)

Silver, Brenda R., *Virginia Woolf Icon* (Chicago: University of Chicago Press, 1999)

Snaith, Anna (ed.), *Palgrave Advances in Virginia Woolf Studies* (Basingstoke: Palgrave, 2006)

Whitworth, Michael, *Authors in Context: Virginia Woolf,* Authors in Context Series (Oxford: Oxford University Press, 2005)

Index